DON'T CALL ME CRAZY

JESSICA RICH

Copyright © 2021 Jessica Rich

Cover design by Jessica Rich

Interior design by David Ter-Avanesyan

ISBN: 978-1-7370920-0-1

All rights reserved. No part of this publication may be reproduced, stored or transmitted in any form or by any means, electronic, mechanical, photocopying, recording, scanning, or otherwise without written permission from the publisher. It is illegal to copy this book, post it to a website, or distribute it by any other means without permission.

Jessica Rich has no responsibility for the persistence or accuracy of URLs for external or third-party Internet Websites referred to in this publication and does not guarantee that any content on such Websites is, or will remain, accurate or appropriate.

Designations used by companies to distinguish their products are often claimed as trademarks. All brand names and product names used in this book and on its cover are trade names, service marks, trademarks and registered trademarks of their respective owners. The publishers and the book are not associated with any product or vendor mentioned in this book. None of the companies referenced within the book have endorsed the book.

Jessica Rich has no responsibility for the health or actions of any individuals other than herself. Any experiences or opinions expressed are solely her own and are not meant to diagnose or treat any illness or ailment.

**FOR EMILY AND BECCA,
WHO HAVE BEEN WITH ME TO HELL AND BACK.**

INTRODUCTION

The first thing I remember is a moment in one of my parents' very earliest little apartments. They had borrowed it from my great-grandparents. I must have been just three or four at the time.

I lay in a pool of golden afternoon sunlight on the living room floor. I remember how warm the sun felt on my skin. I remember the dust motes swirling in the golden light. I remember the musty smell and itchy texture of the ancient orange carpet. I remember the summer breeze coming through the screen of the front door, and staring at its simple metal pattern, letting the tiny sunlit squares form new shapes as my gaze slid in and out of focus.

And I remember the fear. The overwhelming, uncontrollable, incomprehensible anxiety that made my heart pound in my ears, my breath come in tiny gasps, and the orange and yellow room spin around me as I lay comfortably in the sunlight.

Where did the fear come from? Even through the panic of the memory, I can see that the description sounds idyllic. At least, besides the ugly carpet.

And I've thought it through, way too many times. Over and over again. I've looked at it from every angle. I don't remember anything that might have made a three-year-old nervous. The fear came from nowhere. There was no trauma. No trigger. It came from inside me.

I'm not three anymore. I'm a millennial all grown up to my full height of five foot two. I'm still pretty sick. I'm writing from my parents' couch in my dad's old college sweatshirt, listening to Daya in the background.

I grew up in Northern Utah, mostly. It's consummately gorgeous. I adore the slope of the mountains and the smell of pine trees.

I moved to Iowa with my family just in time for high school, and, later, almost got a degree in Idaho. I now, officially, have one in Professional Studies from the same school.

Right now, though, I'm back living with my parents in Iowa, mostly haunting the house with three cats, besides showing up, still in pajamas, for way too many psychiatrist appointments.

I've been sick for a long time. Started around the point of that terrifying sunny memory, when I was three-ish, I think. In a lot of ways, it's all I've ever known.

The book you're holding is about mental illness and life. It's not a textbook overview of clinical diagnoses. I am far from professional. My understanding of mental disorders comes from twenty-five long years of fighting my own brain and watching people I love do the same. And listening to doctors explain what's wrong with me. This is about what it's really like to live and breathe mental illness.

If you're expecting some sugar-coated fairy tale story of how I got better, you're reading the wrong book.

I'm not saying there'll never ever be a happy ending. But if there's gonna be one, I haven't found it yet.

There's a whole lot of stuff out there about people with mental illness. A lot of it's mindless crap. There're the sick Hollywood tragedies about insane war heroes, psychiatrists testing cruel experiments on patients, and ill-fated, violent love triangles that end in romantic suicides. Think along the lines of *One Flew Over the Cuckoo's Nest* or *Romeo and Juliet*. The kind of people behind that trash know nothing about mental health. It's just a source of entertainment, and it does a lot of harm to people with ACTUAL problems. That junk makes me sick(er than I already am).

Then there's the genre of writers without a clue who preach that mental illness is some sort of moral choice. Or a punishment from God or a patient's own subconscious. It's a toss-up whether that or the Hollywood garbage is more damaging.

There are also a whole bunch of no-medication, no-medical treatment cures that are all about confession and contrition, or some new system of thinking, or some diet or magic vitamin. Some of those have a little merit. But I've seen and tried my fair share of "miracle" cures and never met more than one or two that actually accomplished much.

And of course there are the textbooks. Those are usually pretty accurate. If you want the bare scientific facts.

I've heard the facts. I've seen the stats. I've been questioned by dozens of doctors. I've filled out their surveys hundreds of times.

"Please circle the answer that best describes your experience in the past two weeks for the following symptoms: 1 (0-2 days per week), 3 (3-4 days per week), 5 (Almost every day)

Feelings of worthlessness or that you have let yourself, your friends, or family down.

Moving or speaking so slowly that somebody could have noticed.

Thoughts of hurting yourself or somebody else."

I'm long since tired of seeing my symptoms reduced to numbers on a chart. I'm tired of being told to try new things that never work. In my twenty years of fighting my own brain, one thing that's helped enormously is just realizing that I'm not the only one in the world feeling this way.

Despite leaps and bounds in treating mental health like actual medicine, the medical enigma of mental illness is still cloaked in prejudice and misunderstanding. And it really is an enigma. Doctors sort of understand it, but it's a little like Taylor Swift's metamorphosis from country to pop. You can see point A. You can see point B. But you can't QUITE put your finger on what happened in between. It's like somebody took a bare definition of mental illness and eight rolls of duct tape, and wrapped the facts so tightly that it's almost impossible to see them anymore. For the world to make any progress in treating mental illness, the first step is to cut off all the duct tape with little bits of grass and lint and old cat toys and who knows what else stuck in between.

Every single person in the US knows somebody with mental illness. They might not recognize it. But we're talking one-fifth of the country's population at any given time. You know more than five people? Chances are pretty good there are a few mental illness patients in your social circle.

It surrounds us all, whether we know it or not.

So, I'm writing a book. 'Cause I know the downs and the downs (somehow "ups" just doesn't apply). They say to write about what you know, after all. It's gonna sound insane. It's gonna be hard to read sometimes. And I hope that at other times it will bring comfort and faith in a better future. If you want the plain and chaotic truth, it's in these pages.

This is my life.

I'm not offering a solution. I'm not spewing disembodied statistics. I'm not blaming anyone, or worse, trying to romanticize something horrible. I'm just telling it like it is, which is terrifying and dizzying and exhausting and horribly, horribly painful. But not crazy.

Never call me crazy.

Because this is real, as you're about to find out. Welcome to the world of mental illness.

CHAPTER ONE

"MENTAL ILLNESS" IS A TERM THAT GETS USED A LOT, BUT NOT MANY PEOPLE ACTUALLY KNOW WHAT IT MEANS—AND IT MEANS A WHOLE LOT MORE THAN MOST PEOPLE GIVE IT CREDIT FOR. THE WAY THE WORLD AT LARGE USES IT, IT DESCRIBES A SET OF ILLNESSES THAT INVOLVE PROBLEMS WITH HUMAN EMOTIONS AND THOUGHT PROCESSES.

Where did it come from? Well, I know it runs in my family. It's not something I developed at random. It's in my DNA. It's probably been around as long as humans have, for the last few hundred millennia of evolutionary history. It would have come right along with the rest of the diseases that hit the world when Adam and Eve left the Garden of Eden. Or developed alongside every other disease that's followed us through the centuries.

Mental illness has been recorded for thousands of years. It's in the pages of both the Old and New Testaments. It's in other ancient texts. Know what to look for, and it can be found in medical records and censuses going back at least through the middle ages. It's in our stories going back generations.

I've even heard of other species having some of the same problems.

Like a nervous horse responding to daily anxiety medication.

Unlike horses, though, our species relies on multi-layered, intricately crafted, and very confusing social contracts, beliefs, laws, and customs. Our enormously complex social systems reflect the emotional systems that drive them.

Love, lust, anger, compassion, fear, courage, joy, despair, desire, disgust. When I picked up a copy of an abridged dictionary and skimmed through the A section, I found about fifty-five words referring to emotions. They're a basic part of being human, and one that even the most experienced people never completely understand. Every person has to learn to decipher, react to, and control their own feelings, and try to use wisdom while weighing emotional factors against logical ones in making decisions. Our phones even suggest emojis to help us communicate every time we type in an emotional word.

Every culture approaches feelings differently. My white European ancestors have excelled at quashing and hiding emotions for centuries. Children in our society are almost immediately begun on that path. The first time a mother tries to stop a baby from crying.

A lot of people even think emotions are dangerous. The ultimate anti-logic.

Those people are looking at the things that emotions like love, anger, desire, and jealousy inspire people to do.

It is undeniably true, emotions lead us to do some weird things.

Wage wars. Abandon a previous life to start anew on another. Sacrifice our lives, even. But they are also what make us help other people. Save lives. Persist even when things get hard. Write books baring our souls in the hope of helping even just one person feel better about their own life.

There are people who only see the pain in life and try to beat their feelings all to death, thinking it will protect them. That way tends to lead to prejudice, closed-mindedness, and catastrophes like war or murder. And to decades, sometimes even generations, of hard work followed only by the bitterness of a life not truly lived. Some of it inevitably comes from teaching children to suppress and ignore emotion instead of understanding and using it. Some of it is a side effect of unrealistic and constricting gender expectations. Some of it comes from generations of abuse that have been furtively passed down. Some of it simply comes from the experience of everyday pain that is part of life.

Then again, there are others who see only their own desires. Who think they can do whatever the heck they want and never be in the wrong. People who just follow wherever their emotions lead them. Bullying. Screaming matches. Sleeping in 'til noon on a work day. One night stands. Rape. Whatever they feel like. In contrast, this way of life leads to laziness, its own fair share of catastrophes, some incredibly giant temper tantrums, and overall chaos in which nothing ever actually gets done. It tends to end in regret over decades wasted satisfying immediate desires instead of finding actual meaning. This way of thinking comes from overindulgence and being spoiled. It comes from a person being told repeatedly that they can do no wrong. And sometimes from dealing with so much pain that eventually someone gives up on even trying.

Time has proved that neither way works. Maintaining emotional balance is one of the most important skills people need to succeed as human beings. People without it tend to get themselves into trouble.

So an illness that messes with emotions is HUGE.

How does it mess with emotions? Feelings, emotional and physical, are triggered by chemicals in the brain. Mental illness throws off how those chemicals work. It can block the chemicals from taking effect. It can manufacture way too much of a chemical. It can throw around random chemicals out of nowhere. I'm convinced that's what my brain does for fun. "You haven't cried in three hours? Let's fix that."

Those chemicals can also manufacture sights and sounds, even tastes, smells, and physical sensations that aren't real. They can stop the brain from being able to focus on anything. Or make it obsess over one thing alone. They can prevent the brain from forming memories. They can stop it from processing new information and make learning extremely difficult.

Those chemicals are what our thoughts, feelings, and even interactions with the rest of the world consist of. Mess with them, and everything changes.

Even though mental illness has been around for forever, we still don't really understand it. The scientific world now knows about those chemicals in the brain, and can even pinpoint a few of them and summarize what they do. But it's far more intricate and delicate than we understand.

Imagine the universe. Our earth. Our solar system. Our galaxy. Every one of the stars: the ones we can see, and the ones we can't, many with their own solar systems. All those planets. All that space dust. All the life that may exist with its own societies and customs, perhaps more complex than ours, for all we know. All those complicated combinations that we can't even see, let alone comprehend.

And then imagine your brain. Microscopic chemical particles, each with its own triggers and consequences. Breaking apart or combining in endless variations, each with a different effect on your body and mind. Every single thing you have ever thought or done, subconsciously or consciously, is created inside the universe that is your brain. In the same way, we can only see a fraction of what goes on, and understand even less.

In part because of that intricacy, doctors can't reliably treat mental illnesses, though they can take a stab at it and see what happens.

I've been stabbed at more times than I can keep track of, but I'm still plenty sick. And with half the mental health treatments out there, doctors honestly have no idea how they work, just that they get results. Sometimes. Some of those were discovered by accident.

To say the least, the world has a shaky definition of mental illness. It's hard to diagnose. It's even harder to treat.

But I can tell you a few hallmarks. They come from my life, not a textbook.

First of all, it's not normal.

It's normal to feel tired and discouraged after a long week of work that didn't really accomplish much.

It's not normal to be so exhausted on a Tuesday morning that you can't even answer your phone when your boss calls to ask why you're not at work, or to feel so much despair by the end of the week that death sounds relaxing.

Second, emotions caused by mental illness don't respond to reason.

Normally, when someone has a problem, they can sit down and work through it. They think through the pros and cons, do some research, and find the best possible solution. They might feel some fear and worry, it may take some time, but they find a solution that works, go with it, and feel better.

In my brain, on the other hand, I think through the same problem a hundred times, over and over again. I recognize that there's nothing to be worried about, I do what needs to be done, but the feeling never goes away. I'm still terrified long after my half-imaginary problem has been solved.

Third, emotions caused by mental illness don't make sense.

Regular emotions are caused by something. That truth runs all the way back through our evolutionary history from the days when fear followed the moment when the woolly mammoth you were charging turned to look at you. Today, joy might follow when you meet your best friend for dinner after three hours of studying for a test.

Most of the time, my emotions just plain don't fit the situation. And I don't mean the normal girl thing where I'm on my period and my emotions are kind of everywhere and don't always completely add up. I mean that I have an absolutely amazing day where everything goes right: I got an A on that test, I hung out with my friends, I ate my favorite meal for dinner, it's a Friday night, and I should be on top of the world. But I come home, I walk into my bedroom, and I break down sobbing, and if someone asked, I wouldn't be able to tell them why.

And on the reverse side, I can have a day that just spells disaster, score a C on the test, have a bad migraine, an argument with a friend, and a pile of homework I don't want to do, and come out of it without breaking down, at least.

Lastly is something that I catch in myself all the time. The emotion comes before the problem.

In healthy brains, emotion follows a trigger. You feel joy when you see the sun come out, and you feel annoyed when you get a cold.

With mental illness, emotions come out of nowhere without rhyme or reason. I feel terrified. But it doesn't make sense. So, in a split second, my brain searches through all the things that could possibly be causing this feeling and grabs something in desperation to try to make sense of the emotion. It took me years to start noticing this in myself. I'd like to think I can catch it now, but I doubt I recognize it even half the time it happens.

My brain freaks out when it can't explain the fear or the emptiness. So, it lies to me, telling me that I feel horrible because I'm worried about my brother being safe in the Philippines, when actually it's just that my brain's messed up. But then later, if I think it through, the pieces don't quite fit together. There was no chain of thought that led me to that fear. It was just there. It usually happens so fast that I don't notice at first that I feel the emotion before I know the reason. The real reason isn't the one I think it is.

Mental illness is enormously complicated. Those are a few obvious red flags. But it's so much bigger than that. It can swallow you whole. And it's different for every person. But it's very real. Not a figment of imagination. Not a punishment for sin or a way of getting attention. It's physical and chemical. It's enormous. And very, very real.

CHAPTER TWO

IN A LOT OF WAYS, I AM MY ILLNESS. THERE HAS TO BE A DISTINCTION THERE, SOMEWHERE. BUT I'M NOT SURE WHERE TO FIND IT, IF THERE IS. MY SYMPTOMS DEFINE ME AS MUCH AS ANYTHING ELSE ABOUT MY LIFE. AND WHEN I TRY TO THINK BACK, ALL I SEE IS SICKNESS.

The first memory I have, of lying on that carpet in the sunlight, is from when I was just a toddler. Honestly, I don't remember most of my life. Maybe I should say it's been blocked, but actually it's the worst bits I remember . . . I think? I don't really have much to compare them with.

It's more like they've been stolen, those memories. Mental illness sucks the life out of everything. Light, peace, faith, excitement—it destroys everything good.

Just yesterday my parents mentioned something that I did just a year or so ago, that I have absolutely no memory of. And my sister asked me if I remembered much Gaelic. Apparently, in high school, I bought a computer program and started studying the Gaelic language. I love Irish and Scottish history. I can see myself doing that. But, do I remember any Gaelic words? Hon, I can't even remember wanting to learn it. People are constantly telling me about things I've done that I have no recollection of . . . Hopefully I'm not missing anything too important? Who knows? Maybe I eloped and then forgot about it and I still have a secret husband out there somewhere.

Being in constant emotional crisis leaves no room for making memories. Someone running for their life isn't going to remember the daffodils they sprinted past. Every atom in my body is just fighting to keep breathing most of the time. That's all it remembers.

So where did that fear come from?

I have mental illness on all sides of my family. Both my parents and all three of my siblings have some form of it. I just got lucky. The gene jackpot!

That terrified, confused toddler lying in the sun twenty years ago probably would have been diagnosed with a general anxiety disorder. If she had known enough to know it was abnormal to feel that way.

Most health problems are pretty straight-forward. At least in our century. There are tests to diagnose them, and then hopefully a way to fix them, or at least to treat the symptoms. But the lines between mental illness and normal emotions are often vague and difficult to see, especially because a person's first experience with mental illness is frequently caused by some sort of traumatic event.

How do you measure emotional pain?

Most of the symptoms are subjective. There's not some blood test with a clearly-defined line between okay and sick. Even psych specialists have trouble identifying the symptoms and separating one diagnosis from another.

Just a few months ago, I finally saw a psychiatric diagnosis specialist and took a whole bunch of electronic tests that are designed to measure things like reaction time, differences in reactions to auditory or visual stimuli, and a whole bunch of other things I didn't really understand. I was diagnosed with some things I never would have guessed, and some things I had already recognized years ago. But even with that kind of precise data, the doctor had to do some guesswork in order to say what she thought my diagnoses should be.

At this point in my life, with a few diagnoses and a whole lot of meds, I can sort of tell abnormal from normal. I think? But the first life skill I learned was how to hide what I felt, even though I didn't understand that there was anything unusual about me. Not at first.

So it was a long time before I was diagnosed with anything.

But even now, diagnosed with several mental illnesses, I can't usually tell which symptoms belong to which illness. Or separate the symptoms from each other, even. Does fear of people feel different than fear of leaving the kitchen table dirty? And is despair a symptom of depression, or a symptom of anxiety? Which anxiety disorder? I have like, five. I can't keep track of them all.

So I fight each symptom the best way I know, without really knowing exactly what I'm fighting.

By the time I was in kindergarten, I lived with my family in a house with a stream running through the backyard.

I don't know exactly when my social anxiety started. But I know that it was in full bloom by that year, because it was then that I found a dead dragonfly. It was perfectly preserved and its tiny stained glass wings were the most beautiful thing that my four-year-old self had ever seen. Reverently, I put it in an empty pizza box and carried it carefully to school for show and tell.

I was so excited for show and tell that day that I couldn't focus on anything else. Finally, my teacher took the box from me and gestured with her hands as she explained to the class what was inside. As she gestured, the box tipped just enough to let my perfect dragonfly fall to the ground and be crushed under her foot.

I was devastated. Not only from the loss of my treasure, but from the embarrassment of having nothing to show after the buildup in front of my classmates. I cried for days, feeling like the shame of my school. All this over a tiny, dead dragonfly.

My teacher felt so bad that she bought me a little plastic dragonfly. I hid it. Looking at it triggered too much anxiety. I finally threw it away a couple years ago. It still triggered a panic attack even then. Normally, I would have given it to a friend with kids, or to Goodwill for someone else to enjoy. I couldn't bear the thought of it seeing the light of day ever again. I buried it in the bottom of the trash can and hoped I would never have reason to think about it again so that the anxiety it started in the pit of my stomach would be dead and buried with the gorgeous dragonfly from all those years ago.

Social anxiety is the demon that haunts me most. As I continued through the next years of elementary school, I spent many hours pacing up and down that streambed in my backyard, seeking solitude and peace which never came. I still haven't found them.

I spent my school years hiding in the back corners of classrooms, hoping nobody would notice me. I focused on my work. I was one of the best students in most of my classrooms. Except in group projects. Group projects were the literal subjects of my nightmares. Still are. I haven't been in school for two years. Just being in the presence of people still inspires overwhelming terror.

I would rather have peed my pants than raised my hand and drawn attention to myself to ask to use the restroom. Actually, I did. Multiple times. You'd think I'd have learned.

One of those times I clearly remember. I must have been in about second grade. The teacher asked for no interruptions. So I didn't interrupt. Afterwards, sitting in a pool of pee in my seat, I replied, "You said no questions." She rolled her eyes. What did she expect me to do?? Obviously I couldn't raise my hand!

I spent recesses literally building myself a cave of sand underneath a slide so nobody could see me. Either that or soaring so high on a swing that no person without wings could hope to reach me. An added benefit of swinging high and fast was that the wind quickly dried the tears that would have given me away.

Imaginably, I had few friends. Those I did have included me more out of pity than anything. The likability of someone too scared to talk or move with corresponding social and physical skills isn't high.

Thankfully, I found an exception in my extended family, whom I was (mostly) not scared of. All the social skills I learned I owe to my cousins.

Like I said, I don't remember most of my life. I remember a few things, though, from when I was a kid. Just enough to realize my childhood was a bit of a mess.

So much was wrong with me, but by the time I recognized it I just thought I was defect or something. When I was maybe eight-ish, I remember going to my grandma's house one specific time. The day was rainy and dark. I was used to that house being full of cousins, but this time it was just me and my siblings. I liked silence, even then. Noise made me panic. But the dark silence that day was penetrating, it made me feel empty.

It was the stark, melancholy need to be alone that made me step outside into the gray. The rain had stopped falling hours before, but the cold made everything sluggish. The raindrops stuck to the grass like thick sap. The world was soaked in cold gray. I grasped for a reason why I felt so gray, but my mind refused to function. The grass looked black and my bare feet looked as gray as the sky.

I had lots of good times in that yard, giggling with my cousins, but they seemed lifetimes away. The only life that day was the goosebumps stippling my arms. The more I tried to make myself feel better, the less I touched reason.

I stood under a pair of trees. The weeping willow wept droplets of rain while its partner leaked sticky strands of sap. The strands, like a spider's web, floated through the rigid air in ethereal disregard to the water and chill. On the stiff grass at the tree's bed lay dozens of walnuts. A few weeks earlier, they would have been like leather limes, their tough skin green and stiff. The green had turned into black mush that stained toes the color of dried blood, and then disappeared to leave the hard inner shell.

My mind was as numb as my fingers that day. I gathered a handful of nuts from the wet grass and then trudged across the chilled concrete, shoving them into my pockets. The stone wall had dried, but my cold fingertips slipped as I climbed it. The nuts in my pockets dug into my thighs. On the other side of the wall, I chose a few flat stones from a pile and emptied my gritty pockets.

The motions were ones I had repeated dozens of times, but they seemed like part of another world. My fingertips were far away. I was huddled cross-legged on the stones, but my body didn't touch the ground or the air. I could see reality, but it was far out of reach. I was an alien, looking down unfeeling and unknowing on my own existence. The harder I tried, the blanker my mind became, as if the cold that numbed my fingers seeped into my brain, desensitizing every thought. If I let myself stop moving, I felt panic pooling in the corners of my mind and frantically, I searched for a reason— any reason. The emptiness barely masked a fog of unreasoning anxiety that seeped into every pore. My hand trembled as it lifted and dropped the rock, and the walnut split with a crunch and the ringing of stone on stone.

My fingers picked through the bits unsteadily, finding tiny splinters of flesh amid the shards, but my teeth felt more grit than nut.

The grind of my teeth on black shell and the woody taste of walnut belonged to another person. My body moved mindlessly, nut after nut, seemingly forever. My shaking fingers chose a nut, then placed it gingerly on a bed of rock. A heavy stone rose to my eyes and cracked down on shell and stone, the hollow sound cutting through the gray air like a blade. No knife could penetrate the fog in my mind. It was always there.

It still always is. But that day it threatened to swallow me.

Somehow I had lost control. I had become the numbness, or the numbness had become me. I searched for logic, jerking drunkenly from fragment to fragment, but nothing made sense.

There was no reason, but there must be a reason. If there is no reason, then the reason is me. If there is no reason, then somehow I am one with the fog, the panic, the thickness that depresses every one of my thoughts and actions.

That oneness with the numb and the fear. Identifying more with a cold stone block than with a person. It's one of the oddest sensations mental illness has to offer.

Still my movement continued, methodical and silent except for the sound of colliding stones. With every walnut was a reason to feel so numb. And like the fragile nut, every reason was crushed under my hand. Over and over, until every nut was gone and the shards lay scattered around me. Because I knew the conclusion I would come to, somewhere deep in the fog. It's me. The only real reason. The fog, the panic, the anxiety and the loneliness. It comes from the darkest corners of my mind. No matter what I do, it's in there, lurking like an enormous hound turned on its owner.

We are one, the violent dog and its cowardly master, the helpless nut and the hand that crushes it. Which part I play it doesn't matter, because they are the same. It is me, and I am it. Somehow I was born to this. Somehow I am inferior, to be one with an innate reservoir of filth, of fear and shame. I hate the darkness that overwhelms me, but I hate myself more. Because I am the darkness, and never can I escape myself. Forever, I will be like the walnut, shattered, uncomprehending and loathsome, under my own hand.

I felt it then, as a child. I didn't even begin to understand it. I knew that the way I thought was messed up somehow. I knew that I was doing something wrong, I just didn't understand what it was. It's hard to fight an unknown enemy, and harder to fight one within your own borders. I hid it because I was ashamed of it. And because I didn't understand it. How would I explain something I couldn't understand?

The experience I had that day was common. It still is. Luckily, I understand it enough now to fight it, but I can't stop myself from feeling it. Like that day, overcast days are often the hardest for depression. They still make me feel numb and far away. When the sun peeks out between the clouds, I run to stand in the light for a few minutes. And even though I logically know now that I'm feeling depression symptoms, I still can't draw the line between me and it.

I remember another day in particular. I was in eighth grade, sitting in history class.

Class started at the bell. I hated that bell. It signaled the heart-racing battle through the halls, the start of every period that took all of my strength, and even the long and anxious bus ride home. As class began, the teacher explained the worksheet due at the end of class. He pointed out a stack of laminated maps in the back of the room.

Relief flooded through me. No discussion, no hand-raising, no eye contact required, just a simple assignment. I sped through the worksheet, but toward the end, I hit some questions I couldn't answer. My classmates began one by one retrieving maps from the back of the room.

And still I sat at my desk, wrestling with the choice before me. I couldn't stand up. The attention of the entire class would be on me. Fear constricted my throat and I started breathing heavily. I was running out of time. My heart beat faster and I clenched my clammy fists inside my pockets. I should have stood up earlier, by this time I would stand out even more. But I had to have a map.

Finally, I stood. My heart was beating in my throat. I walked slowly, one painful step at a time, conscious of every move, every breath. At the back of the room, I made a weak pivot, my eyes glued to the ground. I slid into my seat with relief and took several minutes to calm my breathing before using the resented map to complete the last few questions of my assignment.

Social anxiety has always been the clincher on my stack of mental illnesses. It's always been the hardest. It probably always will be. Of course, it's hard to tell which illness is which. But my fear of people is the one that controls my life most.

When I was about six, there was one summer when the only shoes I wore for three months were sandals. In the fall when I had to put my tennis shoes on again, I had forgotten how to tie them. I tried, but I couldn't figure it out. I sat on the bench in my garage in the sun staring at those shoes, trying to decide if I should go ask my mom to show me how. But I was too embarrassed. EVERY six-year-old could tie their shoes. I couldn't ask.

Instead, I spent a solid hour experimenting with my shoelaces until I had invented something that looked like a crooked bow. It looked close enough that nobody ever noticed until I was in college. I still tie my shoes weirdly. And one side always comes undone. Because I was too anxious to ask for help when I was six. But, hey! I invented a new type of knot! That's gotta count for something.

The summer before my freshman year of high school, my family moved from Utah to Iowa. I was pretty bitter. It didn't help that in our new house, I had to share a bedroom. One with a curtain for a wall. My sister was excited to share a room with me but I fought and fought my parents about it and cried a whole lot when I had to do it anyway. It made my sister feel pretty bad about herself, which I still feel sorry for.

What none of us, including me, realized, was that the reason I needed my own room was that I desperately needed a private place to hide where I didn't have to feel any social anxiety.

I'm still not a Midwest fan. Humidity, corn, soy beans, football rivalry, water towers, and did I mention the humidity?

It was that year, my first year of high school, when I was first diagnosed with mental illness. Ironically, it was depression. Anxiety has always been my bigger problem. I think I had depression before, but that first year in Iowa, away from my cousins and the mountains, made it much, much worse.

Being diagnosed with anything was a huge step for me, though. The first one in a long, long, trek. Instead of just feeling like a complete freak, I at least had something to explain WHY I was a complete freak. I started medications and therapy. I was really sick. And I've mostly gotten worse since then, honestly, though the last couple years have had some ups and downs. But at the same time it was the first time I felt any hope.

Maybe I'm not just a freak? Maybe I can get better somehow?... Twelve years later, I am now finally seeing a little bit of improvement. It's a long way still to go, but I'm gonna keep fighting for it with every bit of energy I have, for the rest of my life if I have to.

I fought then, too. I did some important stuff. I was named the second best high school artist in Iowa my senior year. I excelled in every subject (except PE; I'm still an overweight, unathletic klutz), and I graduated as valedictorian. I held leadership positions at church, and I spent most nights working hard on homework until early morning.

I also cried a TON, constantly fought overwhelming fear, tried a few dozen medications and several therapists I hated, and made a few people mad at me for always blaming everything on my mental illness.

After I graduated high school, I started my freshman year at a church school in Idaho as a biology major. After that first semester, I changed my major to art education. I tell people it's 'cause I got my first ever B+ in pre-calculus that semester, which is true. But I also got a B in chemistry, the difference being I love stoichiometry and hate calculus. I guess any major that requires calculus knowledge isn't for me?

The real truth is I couldn't handle the stress of those B+'s and I knew I would spare myself some serious anxiety through college by switching to something I knew I could always get straight A's in. I could have excelled at biology, but there would've been a few B's sprinkled into my record, and I just didn't need any more anxiety.

It was also that first semester that I first felt truly suicidal.

And lost someone I thought was my best friend because of it.

I should probably clarify that I've wanted to die since I was little. But it was always just sort of a background, sarcastic wish. I had even self-harmed for years without realizing what I was doing. I guess, because I was so little, and didn't even know what depression was, let alone self-harm or suicide, I just never recognized it. It was that semester that I actively thought about actually, purposefully, hurting myself.

And I kept getting worse. Until I was barely keeping up in classes and it took all my energy just not to kill myself.

It was three weeks before my graduation with a bachelor's degree that I was suspended from school because I had called out for help from my roommate when I was standing with a noose around my neck trying to convince myself that life was better than death.

Which is where I am now, as I write. Kicked out of school for asking for help when I needed it. Trying all sorts of new treatments, hoping that I can somehow get well enough to work or go back to school. And hoping that if/when I do get better, I find a person who I like under all that sickness, because my whole life I have only been my illness.

CHAPTER THREE

YESTERDAY I HEARD THE WORDS "BUT I'M KIND OF OCD, YOU KNOW?" FROM THE PULPIT AT CHURCH. I WAS ABOUT HALF A BREATH FROM RUNNING UP THE AISLE, HEELS AND ALL, AND SLAPPING THE GUY, SCREAMING "OCD HURTS!!" LUCKILY, MY TWENTY-SIX YEARS OF SURVIVING MENTAL ILLNESS HAS GIVEN ME A RIDICULOUS AMOUNT OF SELF-CONTROL, AND NOBODY GOT EMBARRASSED. OR SLAPPED.

Mental illness is indescribably painful all on its own. I could really do without the dozens of misconceptions and prejudices that make it so much harder.

Not long after I started college, I decided to get a cat. The school gave me permission to keep an emotional support animal. My friends helped me pick her. She's a shelter cat, a tiny little calico: bright-eyed, beautiful, and as sassy as they come.

As odd as it might seem, choosing her was one of the best decisions I've ever made.

I still got worse. And worse. I still ended up dragged from my apartment in handcuffs like a criminal. I still got kicked out of school.

But at least every time she walks up to lick my nose or steal the pen I'm trying to use, there's a genuine at least half-smile in it for me. I don't have many of those.

Now, back living with my parents, I tend to keep track of her in the back of my mind most of the time. I'll find myself out driving to an appointment thinking, "Where is my cat?!" before realizing, duh, she's back at the house. Because she calms my anxiety a lot. I get nervous when she wanders off and falls asleep on another floor of the house. I get even more anxious when she looks up at me with her giant eyes and meows to be let out onto the back porch.

It's fully screened in. She's only twenty feet further away from me. But there's a wall of humidity and heat that makes me sick between us. I have to decide, do I want to be more nauseous and risk this migraine getting worse, or do I want to go get a little less anxious by coaxing her to lick my finger?

I got a lot of weird looks, too, though, back at school. No animals were allowed, except medical ones.

I had a few uncomfortable apartment managers, even after semesters of knowing each other. I mean, we're talking about ME here. I freak out when there are three crumbs on the kitchen counter. If my cat hasn't had a bath in over three weeks, you've got bigger problems to worry about. Like me. Dying, probably.

Having the cat forced me to give my roommates the reason I needed her. It's a story I hated telling to a new group of strangers every few months. I got really good at rattling off a dispassionate, slightly downplayed list of mental health problems and vague ways in which the cat helps. I made one or two good friends that way. The ones who sympathized instead of judging.

But I also for sure had some roommates who always looked at me a little strangely and left the room when I walked in.

Who wants to live with the crazy girl, right? Even if there is an adorable cat in the bargain?

I've always tried to be open about being sick, since high school when I was diagnosed. In my fourteen-year-old mind, depression was just another illness. I was happy to have been diagnosed with something. I innocently thought everything was about to get better. I'd barely even heard of mental illness when I got that first diagnosis. I knew about the physical illnesses that had killed my grandpa. But I hadn't even been introduced to mental illness, let alone the fact that it ran in my family. It might have been nice to know what I was getting myself into, opening my mouth about my mental health. But, then again, maybe if I had known that the world was so prejudiced, I would still be trying to fake it.

I know a lot of people are weirded out by how open I am about my mental health. People who seemed to like me all the sudden start avoiding me. People who treated me normally before they knew start inserting useless platitudes into all our conversations. The ones that really hurt, though, are the ones who roll their eyes whenever I mention being sick.

Mental illness is often hidden. I don't use a wheelchair. I don't carry insulin. I don't have a bumper sticker . . . What I do have is a lot of pain, really bad social skills, a few scars if you look carefully, and a very cute cat.

Invisibility doesn't make my disability any less real. Yes, there are things I can't do. Like make it to your party. Like hold a job. Just because you don't see a sign on my back doesn't mean it's not valid.

In a lot of ways social anxiety makes me invisible. Hiding from society.

There are lots of disabilities out there. Visible and invisible both. Other people struggle with them, too.

But what no patient of a purely physical illness understands is the disbelief in people's eyes.

What makes panic attacks any less valid than asthma attacks? Why is it so easy to think that people with mental illness are just lazy and attention-seeking? Is it fear of the reality that emotions can't always be controlled? Is it the Hollywood hype that paints people like me as violent, evil psychos? Is it the inability to understand? Or is it just the basic human belief that anything different is bad?

The same employer who would gladly give me a day off for stomach flu thinks I'm imagining the panic that's making me hyperventilate in the back room.

A teacher who would cut some slack for a student struggling with grief refuses to consider that my depression could be hurting my grades.

And the "friend" who would bring ice cream and a chick flick if I had a cold won't talk to me when I need help because my pain is emotional, not physical.

"Friends" like that don't last long with me.

The classifications we've put on mental health may be useful as far as treatment goes, but they only hurt people when we try to apply them to anything bigger.

Sleep disorders are sometimes classified as mental disorders because they affect the brain and brain chemistry. I don't know enough about sleep disorders to be able to make a decision about where they should fit. I'm not exactly a doctor. I do know that one of the rarer symptoms of narcolepsy, a sleep disorder, is hallucinations, and it's sometimes misdiagnosed as schizophrenia for that reason.

But I was reading a website about it, and on a so-called "list of things you should know" about narcolepsy was included "Narcolepsy is not a mental illness!" Exclamation point and all.

I saw red for a couple minutes.

I know narcolepsy comes with its own set of stereotypes and prejudices. I know it can't be easy.

But, seriously?!?

Clarify that some of those scarier symptoms are rare. Refute your own stereotypes. Give stats. Say you're not nuts, I don't care.

Don't try to pretend that the actual experts have come to an agreement on the useless and barbed classification of "mental" or "physical" illness. Don't just disavow an entire group of people and try to throw all the made-up mud on them. Don't tell me you don't know that the stress of narcolepsy means it's often co-morbid with depression and anxiety disorders, so you're throwing it back on your own. Stop spitting out the words "mental illness" like they're a curse!

A couple hundred years ago, just about anything out of the ordinary (especially in a woman) could disgrace an entire extended family. One black blot on a family tree could ruin prospects in life for children, siblings, cousins…

The whole family would spend money and influence to desperately cover up a situation gone wrong and sweep it under the rug rather than face the consequences.

Elizabeth Bennet, in Pride and Prejudice, mourns after her sister elopes, not only for her sister, but because she believed that nobody would ever marry her or her three other sisters. She believed her whole family to be ruined, even though every available man in the family was off searching for her sister.

Mental illness was one of those situations gone wrong.

It's no coincidence that we have as many modern terms for "crazy" as for "Black" or "scarlet woman," all things that have been historically in need of a new way of phrasing every couple of years as the old term became too scandalous to be used in polite white company.

We've come a long way since then. At least most of us have. For the most part, one person's actions don't ruin the chances in life of their whole families. We've learned to be a little more forgiving.

But mental illness is still being swept under the rug. People with illnesses in a gray area like sleep disorders are scrambling to avoid the scandal of being classified with the rest of us crazies.

I don't freaking care where sleep disorders or Alzheimer's are classified.

Actually, scratch that. I do.

Because I'm tired of being swept under the rug. I'm tired of blaming things on my migraines when actually I'm hiding in the dark trying desperately to stop panicking for no reason. But people will still meet my eyes if I say "migraine."

There is NO. SUCH. THING. as "physical" and "mental" illnesses.

Last time I checked, my brain was part of my body, too. Inside my skull. Connected by nerves. And blood vessels. Like everything else.

For the purpose of simple classification, of course, we have to call it something. "Mental illness." "Psychiatric disorders." Whatever you want.

But we have to stop treating it like it's in a different universe to every other type of illness ever. I mean, seriously, the geriatric clinic and the endocrinology one don't get this type of prejudice. They're just different types of health. In fact, I'm not one hundred percent sure

I even know what those words mean.

I think sometimes mental illness scares people. I have enough faith in human nature to believe that most people don't purposely disregard it as a real problem. But they still do it.

It's easy to be scared of things you don't understand. And it's hard to understand an illness that affects emotions first and body second. People are used to bruises and twenty-four hour viruses. It scares them to think that something could affect their emotions the same way.

Emotions are fickle enough as it is. That loss of control is terrifying. I gave up expecting mine to follow any sort of logical pattern ages ago. I just expect it to be bad, and every so often I'm pleasantly surprised when it's a little less bad.

It's also really hard to measure emotional pain. Everyone has bad days. Everyone feels heartache and grief. It's hard for people to believe that simple brain chemicals can make someone feel that same level of pain. It's easy to disregard something when you can't understand its cause.

Pop culture makes the problem worse. That I can't forgive. Twisting a real, medical, and heart-breaking problem to make money. Shakespeare did it. Romeo and Juliet? OBVIOUSLY, suicide is enormously romantic. Never mind that it's a symptom of something real that causes pain beyond most people's understanding. To be fair, Shakespeare wouldn't have known what mental illness was. Not in any terms we would accept today. But that doesn't excuse the generations since who keep celebrating something morally sick. And don't you dare breathe the word "classic." Yeah, it's a classic. Classic trash. No amount of "culture" is worth belittling the level of terror and agony and self-degradation that causes suicides in real life. Ones almost always linked to mental illness.

Somebody mentions Suicide Squad two rows down and I start to panic. People can't just throw that term around! It's not bold and honorable, it's not romantic, it's not brave! It's a word that triggers grief and self-hatred for an enormous number of people who just hide it. Out of fear. Fear of the thing itself. Fear for their families. Fear that they'll be carted off to psych hospitals.

And the number of horror shows that take place in haunted psychiatric hospitals? I've been forced to spend time in those. There's an enormous amount of pain there. But people with mental illness are no creepier than anyone else. Very, very, very few people with mental illness will ever become violent toward anyone other than themselves. So why do they feature as villains in so much revolting entertainment?

By far the most common psychiatric disorders are mood disorders: depression, bipolar disorder, anxiety disorders. Research has been very inconclusive about whether mental illness is linked to violence at all. If it is, it's almost exclusively NOT mood disorders. It's things like extreme psychotic disorders and some types of personality disorders. Even then, it seems very possible if not probable that things like substance abuse, poverty, exposure to violence in childhood, and other factors are skewing results.

It's true that some rarer types of mental illness really do come with scary symptoms. Not just scary for the patient.

Symptoms like manipulation. Or abuse. Those types of illnesses are EXTREMELY rare, compared to the body of other mental illnesses that affect people. But even those illnesses are still illnesses. People who deal with them can still benefit from treatment. And prejudice isn't going to help, either. Instead, we need to educate people about recognizing, avoiding, and ending toxic relationships, whatever type they might be. Prejudice is never the answer.

"OCD" isn't just a trendy descriptor for the way you like to stick to a schedule. It's very, very real. You can't just use it like it doesn't hurt.

Sometimes I think that people still believe that patients of mental illness symptoms are possessed by the devil. A few actually do, ridiculous as it is. But a surprising number of people just still have a leftover belief that we're connected to evil somehow.

They think I just make up my symptoms for attention. I have ulterior motives. I'm using it to excuse laziness. Or I'm just too lazy in the first place to control my own emotions. I pretend to be sick to get the prescription meds because I'm an addict. I've even had the doctors supposedly prescribing the meds take that view. Or I just lack the self-control to manage my feelings like a responsible adult and I could start strangling people at any second.

I've seen every one of those beliefs in action. But I think I can safely say that witchcraft has absolutely nothing to do with my symptoms.

Sloth? You don't know what hard work is until you're fighting with everything you have just to pick up a pencil and keep going when every cell in your body is exhausted and sick when you've only been awake for half an hour but you have no other choice.

And violence? Yeah, I get violent sometimes. I throw my poor stuffed animals at the wall at three in the morning when I'm too anxious to sleep and I hate myself for being awake, like it's a crime. I berate myself for hours over that harmless act that nobody will ever even know about . . . Pretty sure my stuffed panda bear is never gonna press charges, though. The only person who suffers from my "violence" is me.

To some level, I think that established psychiatric practices are part of the prejudice problem as well. I've been seeing psychiatric doctors for more than a decade. And I've seen dozens.

One example is the psych world's official opinion on therapy. I started therapy when I was first diagnosed with depression as a high school freshman. It's like somebody taking a sharp stick and prodding all the places that hurt until there's so much pain you just collapse and cry.

Studies show that a combination of talk therapy and medication is usually best for mental illness patients. I've been to a solid half dozen therapists in passing, and a few I've even stayed with for a year or two. And I've never experienced anything but pain. But I still get psychiatrists who bug me about seeing a therapist every time I go in.

I'm not saying therapy doesn't have a place. I'm saying its place is different for every person. Therapy is not the cure-all that a surprising number of psychiatric professionals see it as. It helps a lot of people with mental illness. But it's only one option in a sea of choices. Me? I get a whole lot more help from klonopin and talking to my best friend than talking to someone who I'm paying to ask me painful questions.

They say that for patients who don't do as well with therapy, it's just a matter of finding the right therapist. Someone you work well with. And then they say that the first few weeks, or months, are never fun, and just to keep at it until it feels better, but it will get better.

I have been to way too many, for way too long to actually believe that.

The last time I chose to go to a therapist, for a specific PTSD problem, I was given a packet of pretty standard negative thinking patterns and asked to identify a few of them in myself, write them down, and return it. I chose not to. Not because I didn't want to cooperate. Because, at the risk of sounding completely full of myself, I have been identifying and often changing most of those thinking patterns in myself since I was in elementary or middle school. Before I had even been diagnosed. Before I had a clue what mental illness was.

It can be incredibly difficult to see yourself or the world clearly from inside severe mental illness. One of the reasons having a therapist can be very helpful. That is a problem I've never seemed to have, though. Instead, I see and overanalyze everything. Especially my own thoughts. So obviously I was going to catch my own thought patterns and start changing them a long time ago. It didn't fix much for me because in my case most of my illnesses are genetic. I already have a therapist in my head. I don't need any more.

What I'm saying is not every patient needs a therapist. If you've tried it a few times, don't let someone bully you into it if it doesn't help. And the same with any other treatment. Listen to the doctors, try it, but don't be bullied or blinded, because unfortunately, prejudice exists among health professionals too. Not just to patients, but to treatments that have yet to be explored. Mental illness may be the most individualized malady in the world, with every single case unique. And yet it may be one of the most stereotyped, even among professionals, who try to treat each case the same way.

The American Board of Psychiatry strongly encourages every patient diagnosed with certain mental illnesses to be attached to a licensed therapist at all times. If this is so important, how come they don't put pressure on other severe illness patients to do that? Therapy is meant to offer support and teach patients to manage their symptoms. It's a tool that should be tried before chemicals in the event of mental illness or trauma, because it's less dangerous. But EVERY person with a life-altering disease needs help finding positive ways to handle their symptoms and their grief and despair and struggle. A trained therapist is just as relevant to a cancer patient as to a depression patient. I imagine they need some help controlling the chemicals in their brains too.

Meanwhile, the world outside psychiatry sees people who use therapy as anything from being so unlikeable that you have to pay your only friend, to being so emotionally weak that you have to go cry to someone every three days.

I've tried dozens of different treatments. A lot of those have stigma attached, too. Like chiropractic methods, essential oils, and self-help books.

ECT is a big one. Electroconvulsive therapy. "Shock treatment." Yes, it's that thing you see in horror films with the patient bolted down to a table, a gag stuffed in their mouth to mask the screaming, and a mad doctor shooting electricity through their brain. Yes, I've done it. Many, many times. Actually, it's one of two things that've ever really helped my depression. And there's no screaming involved. Usually. Though some patients are still just as scared as before any other procedure, and many have severe anxiety disorders on top of that. Once in a while, someone will break down because of the IV needle or the oxygen mask.

One of the saddest places to see prejudice is in doctor's offices. I've had doctors who've treated me like the most important person in the world.

And I've had doctors who've walked into my procedure room, circled around my bed greeting every other doctor, nurse, and student in the room with a handshake, and then reached down to yank the socks off my feet without even meeting my eyes.

Hon, you may think I'm a lab rat. You may think I'm just one more string of letters on your list of procedures to get done today. But, believe it or not, I'm a person. Sick, yes. But still a person. And touching my ticklish feet, especially with no warning, is a really good way to get kicked in the face. If you're gonna treat me like a piece of meat, I might not even feel that bad about it.

I've seen psychiatric professionals brush it off when my symptoms don't quite match what they think my diagnosis should be. I've seen them insist on pursuing a certain line of inquiry or treatment when

I can provide a logical reason why I would prefer another viable option. While there are many good and respectful professionals practicing psychiatry, there are also many who treat their patients like we are completely incapable of making our own decisions, coming to rational conclusions, holding intelligent conversations, or discussing our own diagnoses and treatments. When I run into those kind of professionals, I often make a point of making the most educated conversation I can just to see the scramble to catch up.

It's certainly true that mental illness can affect how well I can keep up, but that doesn't mean I can't make my own decisions, or that I can't be rational. Just that I need a bit of extra support in doing it.

Even the people who I would expect to have the most sympathy sometimes don't. Patients sitting in psychiatrists' waiting rooms. All waiting for the same thing. And yet, there are still furtive, judgmental glances from some patients at the guy with scars running down his arm. Or the girl so thin her ribs stick out through the back of her shirt. They think, "I would never do that." And they stare. And then three months later they find themselves in the same situation and they get mad at all the people judging them.

It's so, so wrong.

But as long as people know about my mental illness, I will get judged for it.

In their eyes, I'm imagining it. It's all in my head. Or I'm just lazy. Or crazy. Or a witch. Or not trying hard enough. Or violent and dangerous. Or even a prescription drug addict.

I mean, seriously, how far do you have to go to convince yourself I'm a liar? I would think an anxiety disorder is a lot more believable than devil worship, but sure, yeah, okay.

The truth is, I'm just a really sick girl trying ridiculously hard to keep up some semblance of a normal life through my very real pain.

So, yeah. It's all in my head. Inside my brain where the wrong chemicals are produced, and receptors are blocked, and things get so out of balance that every function in my body is messed up.

Stop classifying my illness as different from all of the others. It's not. Get over it. Stop stereotyping me. Stop running away. Grow up. This isn't the 1700s anymore. Stop sweeping me under the rug like a speck of dust you're too lazy to put in the trash or too "moral" to burn at the stake like a proper witch. I'm not a stain on anyone. And neither is my illness.

At least my cat only judges me for being human and not for being sick.

Why live when you feel dead already?

CHAPTER FOUR

WHAT DOES BEING DEAD FEEL LIKE?

I guess that's a question nobody will really know the answer to until it's too late to share with the class.

I say I feel dead. There's not really a better way to describe it. The numbness that comes with depression. I don't think it's very accurate, though . . . I believe in life after death. And what is life without emotions? I think our emotions are the first thing we'd retain.

I don't know what death feels like. But I can answer the other question.

What is life without emotions? It's weird, is what it is. Disorienting. Boring. Is bored an emotion? Or a lack of emotion? And it's scary. When I finally realize I'm not feeling anything. And then I sort of know I should be scared, and there are little flashes, but mostly just a cloud hovering over the back of my mind telling me I should be terrified, but somehow I can't seem to muster the fear.

Not that I've tried very hard.

I've heard people say they'd rather feel pain than feel nothing at all.

I'd take the emptiness any day. I do, actually. Maybe it's wrong of me, but I'd rather be empty than terrified. I cultivate the nothingness, sometimes. Times when I know the alternative is a panic attack or hours of tears.

I've never drunk anything stronger than Mountain Dew, but I imagine depression feels very similar to the numbness alcoholics are addicted to. An absence of pain. And, incidentally, everything else. My brain just gets there without help from drugs.

That's what depression really is. It's not the sadness or the terror. Those are just . . . side effects? Depression is like being a walking zombie. No emotions. No physical pain, even, sometimes.

Our brains register physical and emotional pain much the same way. Depression blocks it all. What's left over is just exhaustion and a hollow space where I should be. Once in a while, flashes of sadness or panic or despair break through and they bounce around in the empty space like an echo. It's surreal.

When I'm worst, I don't realize it. I just feel nothing. Comprehend nothing.

I'll be just going about my business until I run into someone else and realize how worried they are. They tell me I'm white as a ghost and shaking and my voice sounds like a drone. And I look down at my hands and something close to surprise almost penetrates. It hadn't even occurred to me.

I'm still pale and trembling. At least some of the chemicals in my brain are still firing. I'm still panicking. I'm still in pain. The signal's just not quite making it all the way through.

Instead, I'm so detached from reality that I don't realize how awful I feel... or don't feel?... until somebody else points it out. And then it's like a slap in the face. That I don't feel. Like watching someone's hand hit me and seeing the view in front of me change as my head moves but not actually feeling the pain.

Sometimes it's those times when I'm furthest from actual life that are the most dangerous.

I'm still suicidal. Without the feelings.

I'll find myself with a knife pressed to my wrist and sort of think "Oh. That's probably bad."

There are so many reasons to die.

Nobody would even notice. It would make the pain go away. The pain is swallowing me whole, there's nothing left that's actually me. And I want to die, so, so badly. In the moments I can feel. Just to get away from the pain and the emptiness and the fear and the judgment and the monotony.

But when I try to make a list of reasons to live . . . The best thing I can come up with is supposedly some people care. I don't actually believe it a lot of the time. But I force myself to keep living anyway. If it even is living. It's mostly just a flat line.

I know the pain is there. Somewhere. I want desperately to get away from it. I think. Will I have feelings again after I'm dead? What will I want? If I could feel now, what would I want?

That's an easy answer. To get away from the pain. That I would be feeling if I could feel right now. That I can sort of feel looming over my shoulder but that disappears if I try to look at it.

The same emptiness that stops me from feeling the pain stops me from feeling the emotions that fight against everything that makes me want to die.

When I can feel, they tear me apart fighting over whether I'm strong enough to keep fighting the pain or too weak to keep living.

When I can't feel, there's nothing to stop me. There's no fight. Just some weird shadows in the corners of my brain that don't quite add up. It's a good thing it's so exhausting. If I wasn't too exhausted to kill myself, I wouldn't be able to feel enough to stop myself.

Logic doesn't really follow in that state. Which way is up? I haven't got a clue. But why keep living and feeling nothing? Isn't life for feeling things? If I can't feel, am I already dead?

Luckily, (supposedly, I still can't find an actual desire to keep living) being too far away to feel anything doesn't really lend itself to action. So instead of dead, I kind of just end up staring at a book not knowing how I got to that page and not knowing what two plus two is. Let alone what I just supposedly spent hours reading.

It can go on for weeks. That nothing. I think. My brain's not really functioning well enough to make memories. I just remember some snippets. Or I find scraps of paper with descriptions of living hell months later. Makes studying for finals great. I don't even remember the whole last month of class, so I'm just gonna hope I took decent notes and relearn everything. Including those drawings of death in the margins. At least I think I learned the stuff in my notes. At some point. It may have just bounced off my brain. I'm not really sure, since, obviously, I don't remember any of it.

And in the meantime, I guess I owe my life to being chronically too numb to think or feel basically anything. Still not sure if that's a good thing. Guess I'm stuck with it, though.

This is what depression really is.

The medical world still doesn't understand it super well. They've narrowed it down to a handful of chemicals inside the brain that seem to be affected. But there are multiple classes of depression meds that attack different problems. Not the same chemical problem from different points of view. Different processes.

There are multiple diagnoses which all basically mean "depression," but have some basic differences so large that psychiatrists can't actually stick them under the same diagnosis. Major depressive disorder. Seasonal affective disorder. Postpartum depression. Prenatal depression. Dysthymia or Persistent depressive disorder. There's even a diagnosis for depression that doesn't clearly fit any of these diagnoses. Atypical depression, or Major depressive disorder with atypical features. Those are just the ones that don't describe bipolar disorders, which also include depressive symptoms. And even with the same diagnosis, the chemical cause of depression in any one person could be multiple completely different things, with no way to find out which it is except by throwing different medication classes at it and seeing if any of them work. Even then, it's completely normal to react to only certain medications in a single class. Meds A, B, C, D, and E are all very close counterparts of each other. In fact, they were developed as off-shoots of each other. But one patient is only going to respond to one of them well, with no way to know which. And that's only one class of medication.

When you get really desperate (as I have been for years) you can take a gene test that tells you which medications might react well with your genome. That narrows it down a bit. But you're still looking at dozens of viable options and often 4-6 weeks before you even notice any benefit, if there will be any at all. And then dose increases. And then complicated combinations, which, if you don't respond to the couple of most basic medications well, you're most likely to respond to. It could take decades of experimentation just to figure out something that works, if anything does.

Depression symptoms include fatigue, lethargy, sadness, emotional numbness, feelings of despair or self-hatred, suicidal thoughts or actions, changes in eating habits, changes in sleeping habits, weight gain or loss, and half a dozen other things. It can make you over-eat or over-sleep just as easily as under-eat or under-sleep. There seems to be not much rhyme or reason to the group of disorders which all have despair, exhaustion, and emotional numbness as major symptoms.

When it comes down to it, depression is an extremely anti-logical experience.

When I get very worst, I become numb, even to physical sensations, to some extent. I'll find a cat scratch on my arm and wonder, "how long has that been there?" because it doesn't hurt unless I think about it really, really hard. Like trying to gather my disintegrated brain into one piece and force it to do something it just . . . can't. Not anymore. I feel . . . missing? Like everything inside me has turned to dust, but despair and terror are still there peeking over my shoulders just waiting to get in. I know they're there. I can even feel a tiny little blip of them once in a while.

It's more strange than anything else. No matter how much time I spend in that state, it still feels alien. The colors around me don't make sense. The edges of the world don't quite fit together. And no matter what's there, clamoring to get in, nothing inside me survives for long. It's a wasteland. Dead.

CHAPTER FIVE

MY FAMILY PRAYS TOGETHER EVERY DAY. WHEN IT'S MY SISTER'S TURN, SHE HABITUALLY STARTS WITH THE SAME FEW LINES THAT GO SOMETHING LIKE THIS: "WE'RE THANKFUL TO BE A FAMILY AND THAT WE CAN ALL BE HERE TOGETHER TODAY. PLEASE HELP EVERYONE WHO IS SICK OR HURT TO GET BETTER. PLEASE HELP EVERYONE TO BE SAFE AND PROTECTED AND COMFORTED. PLEASE HELP US TO GET WHAT WE NEED TO DONE. PLEASE HELP US TO SLEEP WELL AND BE PREPARED FOR THE DAY AHEAD OF US TOMORROW."

Those lines always remind me of my first experience with OCD.

It was a crazy time for my family. I was nine or ten. We had just built a brand new house on an acre of land and planted fruit trees and a giant new garden. My bedroom was in the unfinished basement, and two of my walls were sheets of black plastic stapled to the studs.

I really liked it there. There were wheat fields all around the house, enormous grasshoppers everywhere, and unobstructed views of the mountains on all sides.

This house though, had a stream inside. The contractor who had built the house hadn't done his job, and my basement bedroom was in the middle of an underground river. The first time it flooded, I remember slipping out of my bed to use the bathroom in the dark and landing in two inches of cold water.

From there, things got hard for my family. My parents started fighting the contractor trying to get some sort of help for his mistake, while the water kept showing up on my floor over and over again. My dad drilled holes in the concrete for pumps. I could peek into the holes and watch the water flow just like a stream under the floor. I had to stay home from church once to flip the switch on one of the pumps so it wouldn't start spraying mud-water all over the walls every half hour.

That first time it flooded, my things were scattered on the floor like any ten-year-old girl's, and half of what I owned got submerged. The bottom few inches of the wall studs and my desk legs started growing mold. Most of my toys and things dried out and were fine. But there was one book that didn't make it.

One of my favorite things to do was to make things out of clay. I had an instruction book with all sorts of projects, like cardinals and teddy bears and Christmas ornaments. It was lying on the floor that first time, and it got soaked. All the pages were wrinkled and most of them were stuck together.

I loved that book, so I very carefully pulled the pages apart and most of them came out okay, but a few were so bad that I couldn't read them anymore.

It's dumb, I know. That stupid little book. But I cried over those pages I couldn't read.

After that, I started keeping everything off the ground. Then I started flipping my lamp back on at night to make sure the corners of my comforter weren't touching the floor. And then getting up and walking around the room to make sure everything was piled securely somewhere high, even though I had already checked eight times.

I couldn't shake the image of those torn pages from my mind and every time they filled me with terror. And then it spread to other things. What if my socks fell out of my bed while I was sleeping and got lost? What if my ceramic doll fell from the desk and broke on the concrete?

So then everything had to be piled in the center of high places, so far from the edges that they couldn't possibly fall onto the floor. There was a mountain of things on the center of every surface in that room.

Then I started feeling guilty. My sister was sleeping across the hall from me. Wasn't her stuff important too? Or my cousins' things? Soon my mind was filled with images of someone in China or Australia dropping a crystal vase.

I couldn't bear the thought of anything being hurt.

But people were more important. What if someone got hit by a car? I couldn't do anything about the people on the other side of the world.

It didn't take long for me to end up huddled in the middle of my bed every night doing the only thing I knew how to do. Pray. I still have the words memorized. "Please help everyone and everything in the world to be safe tonight." I don't know how many times I said that prayer. Thousands. It would make me feel better for a few seconds and then I would say it again. And again. And again, and again, and again, until I fell asleep still saying it.

At the time I didn't know I had any sort of anxiety, and I wouldn't have known what OCD was if I was asked. That's what it was, though. Every night.

Luckily, when we moved out of that house and into another, the worst of the OCD went with it. I still have some traces of it, though it's hard to say what's what in the world of anxiety. I know I definitely still do some things that are compulsive, though.

I was recently diagnosed with a specific pattern of autism that might explain some of those OCD-like symptoms.

Nobody I've talked to would ever have guessed that I had autism. It's hugely surprising to me and my family. But that's what the tests say.

The pattern of symptoms I have is unofficially sometimes called a non-verbal learning disorder. Basically, I have a very high IQ when it comes to all things related to words, written or spoken. Higher with written. I can struggle with spoken. But I struggle a lot with other types of learning. Like recognizing body language. Or remembering people's faces. Or reading maps. Might explain why I started having social anxiety symptoms so early on. I can only understand the verbal half of the way people communicate.

The doctor who made that diagnosis immediately mentioned the possibility that being unable to communicate with people effectively might give me an unusual need for control in other areas of my life. Like the ones I so obsessively moderate. I'm a little less convinced, honestly. I've never asked for a doctor to officially decide whether I have OCD or not because it's at the bottom of my list of worries. But it runs in my family. And I know I'm no professional, but my symptoms certainly look to me like a match. Almost TOO good of a match, actually. Almost stereotypical.

So do I have OCD? I certainly did when I was young. Those compulsive, repetitive prayers couldn't have been anything else. I don't know if I do anymore, or if I just have a few anxieties that look similar. Either way, the symptoms are the same.

My need for neatness and artistic perfection started when I was in middle school. I'm not sure where that came from. But to this day, cleaning my room consists of picking up a pair of socks to put in the laundry and moving the book I was reading last night back to its rightful place on the bookshelf.

The things stored in my cupboards, behind closed doors, are carefully organized and labeled. On each box is a bulleted list of its contents. But it's the things not hidden away from view that give me the most grief.

My stuffed animal collection is organized by type of animal and neatly balanced according to visual weight so that it looks like it could be decorative, not just storage. The candles on my bookshelf are perfectly, asymmetrically arranged by color and visual weight.

And the books are not just in categories but in patterns of size carefully checked for aesthetic quality.

On days when I'm already especially anxious, I try hard not to look around the house too much. Most of my family is pretty clean. But if I'm already stressed and I think about it too hard, I end up organizing every surface and straightening every shelf and hiding every possible object that could be considered clutter inside a cupboard or drawer until I'm drenched in sweat and panicking because I can't find a place to put my sister's medicine bottles that live permanently on the kitchen counter. It's a good way to make enemies in a house that doesn't belong to me. Especially living with roommates.

"Has anyone seen my scissors?"

"Uuuhh. . . . Did you leave them on the kitchen table?"

"That's where they go."

"They're in the cupboard."

"What?"

And I steer as clear as possible of any area of the house where my sister's things live, because they consist of chaotic piles on the floor and it makes me anxious just thinking about them.

I NEED aesthetic balance. Matching colors, intelligent value contrast, exact wood tones, and always the most carefully planned balance based on the rule of thirds (essentially meaning, divide your visual space into thirds both ways and stick what you want to be seen at the intersections), with a clear, always asymmetrical, focal point.

Even the smallest thing can become an obsession. Yes, I know that the classical artists and the old masters used symmetry. Symmetry creates an aura of calm, asymmetry of energy. But stick me in a symmetrical room and I start to panic. It makes me feel like the world is closing in on me. It HAS to be asymmetrical, and not just chaotic, accidentally asymmetrical, but intelligently designed asymmetrical.

I also hate smooth, or especially shiny, surface finishes. There HAS to be some sort of visual texture. When I refinish furniture, there are intentional patterns of paint splatter or shading in a different color. And even after a satin finish, I'll go back and rough it up a little with sandpaper so nothing could ever be construed as smooth.

There are so many things. That color has just a little too much green in it, even though nobody else would even notice a difference. The pattern on the fan blades draws too much attention, it shouldn't be there. It makes everything too busy. I can't look at anything printed, like plastic tiling because I immediately pick out the print that's meant to look like stone and automatically calculate how many tiles have actually been designed, how often the design is repeated, and how the sections are being rotated to make the repetition less obvious. My brain has twisted my artistic instinct into an obsession.

Just thinking about my surroundings enough to write this is making my heart race and my breath shake. I'm trying not to look up at the room around me, even out of the corner or my eye. I want to hide every non-decorative object in this house and make sure every decorated surface is aesthetically perfect. Even then, there's always another thing out of place. Instead of attacking the house, I'm going to pretend I don't see any of it, close my eyes, and try to calm down, but it'll take a couple hours now.

I still have a weird need to not let things get destroyed or wasted, too. I think it's left over from those flooding days. When I lived with roommates, every semester they would leave and end up getting rid of things. Stuff like old dishes and unused food. It should have ended up in the trash or at a Goodwill somewhere. But I still can't bear to part with things that could still have use, so instead I have an eclectic collection of other people's frying pans and ottomans and bathroom scales that I just can't bear to lose, even though they just sit in carefully organized tubs hidden beneath a decorative covering in the corner of my bedroom. Under that stuffed animal collection.

Throwing things away is really difficult for me. I know I have too much junk I don't need, but giving things to Goodwill makes me panic.

Thankfully, most of the time, OCD is at the bottom of my long list of worries. I'm a lot more worried about the social anxiety stopping me from going grocery shopping. It's still there, though. It just sort of hides behind everything else.

Those obsessive fears, when they show up, don't go away. Saying the prayer once doesn't make the fear any less. Straightening one thing only leads to straightening another, and another, and another, until I've straightened every object in the house and I'm back where I started, and I'm going to spend another three hours re-straightening everything I've already done. That's what makes it OCD.

I can go through the living room seven times in a row, compulsively straightening things. Every time I walk out I feel a little bit of relief because it feels balanced, but then every time I walk back in, all the sudden something else becomes clutter.

We don't really need that fan, do we? And then I have to refold the blanket on the couch three times in a row until the corners match exactly. Not like they didn't the first time. And then the blinds aren't quite straight and three specks of dust have reassembled on the TV I just dusted twice and it has to be done again. And you can still ALMOST see the spot where the tag was on the lamp, and that outlet cover isn't quite straight, and the gravel outside the window is lumpy, so I end up with screwdrivers and rakes and hoses when all it really needed was three minutes' worth of straightening (if you ask me when I'm not completely freaking out) or nothing (if you ask anyone else in the house).

Eventually, I have to force myself to curl up in a little ball with my eyes squeezed shut, sitting on my hands, with music blaring in my ears so I can calm down. After a while I can open my eyes just enough to see my cat through my lashes without needing to straighten every square inch of the universe.

But. That's just OCD. There are lots of different anxiety disorders. Just like depression, there are many disorders that fall under the umbrella of anxiety disorders, but saying which is which and keeping the symptoms apart gets enormously complicated sometimes.

Anxiety disorders are marked by fear. Fear that doesn't make sense. It shows up in all different situations and all different types.

The most common types are general anxiety, post-traumatic stress disorder, social anxiety, obsessive-compulsive disorder, panic disorder, and specific phobias. That is by no means a comprehensive list, though.

For me, anxiety is the one thing that never, ever goes away.

My depression (mostly) turns invisible in the middle weeks of my ECT cycle. The autism is there, but as long as I stick to situations with written words, I do okay. Even excel, sometimes. The ADHD is there, too. I'll get caught up in something interesting, like an artwork, and my attention will be absolutely singular . . . which, actually, is an ADHD symptom. I don't mind, though, because at that point, all I feel is the tug of the lines under my hands.

And fear.

In the back of my mind. Worry about whether anyone can hear my music through the wall. A vague fear that this painting won't be any good after it's done. Nagging thoughts about that night, years ago now, when my already shattered life cracked in two. The night I got suspended from school.

Social anxiety defines me most. Some people refer to it as a social phobia, but it's unlike any other phobia in how ridiculously common and life-altering it is. The times I feel calmest are the ones when nobody else is around. I have the house to myself for a week. I can do whatever the heck I want, and nobody will ever know. So I paint for hours with music blaring in the background and order pizza.

I'm terrified of people. The way they look at me. The things they'll say to their friends about me later. What they think about me. The judgment. The questions. The questions are the worst. Questions from people who care, about how I'm doing and what my plans are. I panic just at the notion that they might ask.

I've always hated people. Always hid in the corners of the playground. In the back of the classroom. Always put my back to the wall.

I grew up going to church every week. I used to feel a little calmer there than with the random people off the street. At least I knew the people there believed the same things I did and were largely good people.

Then I went to a church school and realized they weren't all quite as good as I'd like to believe. But mostly, I got sicker. Much, much sicker. And I went from sitting in the back corner of the chapel to sitting in the foyer listening but hoping not to be seen. And then listening, standing, back pressed to the wall in the least frequented corner of hallway I could find. And then only staying for the first few minutes. And then not going at all. Not because I don't want to be there. Not because I love God any less. Because the thought of the hugging, and the well-meaning questions, and being surrounded by people makes me panic just thinking about it.

I can sometimes walk through the grocery store without breathing hard. Most of the time, I can manage strangers without too much stress. What are they gonna do to me? Who cares what they think?

It's the people who ring my doorbell hoping to help who make my heart race and my stomach heave.

The people who I KNOW only care about me.

But I'm a wreck. A mess. I've managed to ruin my life and end up too sick to do hardly anything and how do I face up to that?

Even though I know this isn't my fault. Logically. It's just a sickness. It wasn't me who ruined my life.

No. I'll hide. I'll lie. I'll pretend I'm fine and making more progress than I am and then spend three hours after they leave panicking and trying not to puke.

Panic attacks are a type all their own. At least in psychology textbooks. But it's supposedly bad to get a panic attack a few days a week. Like, really bad. I get them several times a day when I'm really bad. Either that, or my life is one giant panic attack.

Sometimes they hit out of nowhere. Sometimes they're triggered by something. Always, they mean unreasoning fear, a racing heart, nausea, dizziness, backing up with my eyes wide staring at NOTHING like it's going to pounce, until I hit the wall and end up slumped up in the corner crying an hour later.

Usually, for me at least, some tiny little thing will trigger it. I'll hear footsteps in the next room over and my social anxiety will kick in. It shoots from background noise to overwhelming fear in a second. Pounding heart. Can't breathe. Can't see. Everything's closing in on me. Terror like I'm about to die. And then a slow slope toward my base level of anxiety again. I've trained myself to be able to calm down a little faster when the trigger is small. When it's actually not, that's a whole other story.

It doesn't go away easily. Even when I can get to a place where I can breathe fairly quickly, I'll stay on edge for the rest of the day. Or week. Until something lets me finally calm down for real. I might not be breathing like I'm running a marathon, but I jump at every little thing and any one of them might set off the barrage again.

So when the garage door opening makes me yelp and stop breathing, where does the panic attack begin and end? I dunno.

The worst ones, though, are PTSD related. I can't breathe at the mention of any sort of psych hospital. When I'm already on edge, anything related to that night when I called for help with a noose around my neck and got suspended for it can send me running. Always thinking about that day. Always crying over something that happened years ago. Always panicking over a memory that I don't even remember straight anymore. It seems so far away. Like I'm watching it from the outside, someone else, not caring, and yet feeling a kick to the stomach every time it crosses my mind. Which is far, far too often.

People who were part of the story will mention something in passing that they would never connect to that day. And it'll trigger that memory anyway and I'll see nothing but the replay for hours.

I almost wish I could just forget that that day ever happened.

I have repetitive nightmares of a certain person arguing with me. Doing exactly what he did in real life. Or just standing over my bed. I'll sit up in the middle of the night thinking he's standing over me.

Sometimes other people just talk about things they know I have PTSD about all around me like either they don't know, even though I've told them, or they just think it's not that bad.

But I'll see the first initial of a name in the middle of a sentence, out of the corner of my eye, and start breathing faster. People start to talk about it and I collapse.

I drive past the local outlet of the place that fired me when I was spiraling down so fast, and I'll be withdrawn for hours without even completely registering why.

I do my best not to think about those things at all, but so many things remind me. A word. A smell. A chore. And once I get started thinking about it, it's almost impossible to stop. Sometimes I'm angry. Mostly I'm scared and sad and ashamed and disgusted and so many other things.

People think that PTSD has to be from some giant, earth-shattering, violent encounter. An attack. Something criminal. I have had PTSD diagnosed from a couple disparate events. Neither of them were violent. They weren't sudden. They were just emotional and long and horrible. That doesn't make them or their aftermath any less intense or real.

Some aspects of that first experience were sudden. I really didn't expect to get fired, even though I probably should have. I had far too much faith in humanity to expect to be hauled off in handcuffs or suspended when I desperately needed help. But it had been months and years coming. It had been months since I had thought a rational thought or felt something positive. It was months' worth of trauma.

Unlike other anxiety disorders, PTSD does get better with time.

Take away the trauma, and it starts to heal. Slowly.

But it was three years later that I contacted the school that suspended me about somehow finishing a degree, and I had panic attacks for days before and days after just about contacting them. I was able to do it. But not easily.

It's greatly to their credit that somebody there heard some of my story and stepped in to make a degree happen. Just that fact helps ease that anxiety some.

But trauma doesn't ever disappear. Twenty years down the road, I may have made peace with it. I may be able to think about those triggers without it hurting. But those things will always be shaping events in my life.

And general anxiety?

General anxiety is exactly what it sounds like. Just worrying about anything and everything and nothing and who knows what, but always. It never stops. No matter what other, more specific fear is playing through my mind on top, it's always there. A fear that I can't put my finger on.

I try to, sometimes. Try to pin it down to something. But that just makes it worse. It's just there. Nervousness in the back of my mind. It's really weird, honestly. Feeling scared and not actually knowing why.

Knowing doesn't make it go away, though. It is always, always there. Some sort of anxiety. Or three. Or five.

CHAPTER SIX

UNLIKE THE MAJORITY OF MY MENTAL HEALTH DIAGNOSES, ADHD IS ONE THAT WASN'T RECOGNIZED WHEN I WAS A TEENAGER.

I started noticing ADHD symptoms under the mess of everything else my brain does for fun probably a couple years ago. And I laughed them off.

To be fair, I tend to laugh off probably more than an honest share of my problems. Because one of them is believing I have problems when there's nothing there. Or at least, believing I believe I have problems that don't exist when they're actually alive and well. Try figuring that one out . . . I'm not sure I follow that sentence, either.

Maybe more often than I think, it actually turns out I'm right about the problems. A while ago, I got a sinus infection. For the first month, I kept telling myself I was nuts and it was just a bad cold . . . Nope. So I started treating it. Then a few weeks later I thought I might have a UTI, but I wasn't sure so I ignored it for a bit. Honestly, after a few months and a couple doctors, I still don't really know what happened for sure. But I think, over about five months, I had a urinary tract infection that turned into a kidney infection. And then, with my immune system even lower than usual after a string of infections and antibiotics, I ended up diagnosed with pneumonia. Trouble is, I think I might have actually had that for months, even as long as a year or so, and just brushed off the symptoms as normal complications of everything else. I still can't get rid of the pneumonia.

You'd think I'd learn . . . And I do. But knowing I have a sinus infection and convincing my parents I need to go to another doctor and get another round of antibiotics are two very different things. And I'm often so anxious and annoyed that I'd rather deal with the symptoms than with another doctor in order to get help. I just have so many symptoms that never seem to go away. How do you figure out which ones are antibiotic-worthy and which ones are just my arsenal of trash? Nobody else knows, either. Including the doctors. So I just hang out with a sinus infection for a month.

Or, you know, slowly realize I have ADHD and just live with the knowledge for a couple years before I finally work up the courage to convince my unbelieving doctors and family that I need to get tested.

Why were they so unbelieving?

I think the basic answer is that my anxiety is a whole lot stronger than my ADHD.

My youngest sister, who also has both ADHD and anxiety, is always telling me that my ADHD and hers are opposites. I don't believe that. I just think that her ADHD is her bigger problem, while my anxiety is mine.

A lot of the trademark symptoms of ADHD are polar opposites of my social anxiety symptoms. The longer I think about it, the more I realize that I have had ADHD a long time. Since I was a kid.

ADHD can make you fidget and move constantly. Social anxiety can make you suppress every movement.

In a situation where I feel less anxiety, I'm constantly moving. I can't sit and watch tv and ONLY watch tv. I'm twisting my hair into knots—something my parents have been trying to get me to stop since I was in elementary school. Or, I'm rubbing my feet together and giving myself rug burn from my socks. Or picking at my skin. Or playing games on my phone. Or fiddling with a pair of magnets that lives on my table for that express purpose. Neatly hidden in a decorative jar, of course.

But someone enters the room and I go stone cold still. I can't show emotion. I can't draw attention to myself by moving. I can barely breathe. So who sees me moving? Almost nobody.

ADHD can make you talk incessantly. Social anxiety makes you freeze up and never utter a single word.

The very few people I'm sometimes comfortable around know I can talk like crazy. What should have been a five word explanation turns into a text that's five inches tall. Sometimes people think that I'm a little set in my ways because I have a four point argument for anything I say. Actually, I have a four point argument for the other side, too. My brain just has to analyze all the possibilities and reasons. But with the ninety-nine percent of people I'm not that comfortable with, I'm always the quiet one. Not 'cause I have nothing to say. Because I'm terrified to say it. So I keep my mouth shut.

ADHD can make people impatient. Believe me, patience is not my strong suit. When the teacher asks for an answer, my social anxiety makes me wait ten seconds so I don't seem like a total jerk. And then my patience runs out and I just give the answer in the most succinct way possible in order to sort of appease my anxiety by not talking TOO much.

Come on, people. Can we not waste class waiting for answers, please?

ADHD can make you impulsive. And I am impulsive, let's be real. Just not in ways that I could get judged for. Started reading a book last night. Twenty three pages in . . . Eh. Time for a new one. I already predicted the ending anyway. Same with art projects and food preferences and new hobbies to try. And random, alternative medicine experiments. Thankfully, some of those actually work. Who sees those? Well, my family sees that I go through hobbies and TV shows quickly.

But the things that usually draw attention for impulsivity? Splurging money. Changing plans at the last second. I can't do that stuff, however much I might want to. My anxiety would tear me apart.

One of the big things that makes ADHD hard to cope with is lack of organization and time management, which often are factors in making it difficult to keep up in school. I see those symptoms every day in my sister, who has worse ADHD than I do.

ADHD can vary in intensity between visual and auditory senses. I know from diagnostic testing that my attention skills for hearing are twice as bad as my attention skills for seeing. Plus I see it every day. Combine that with a type of autism that manifests essentially as a learning disorder which makes it difficult to process any information not presented as words.

To understand something, I need to see it, not hear it; in words, not graphs or symbols or even pictures, as strange as it seems for an artist. If I can write it down, I'm good. I'll remember it for about three weeks, and then I'll forget it and move on to something new. That's how I got through school so well: see it, copy it, remember it just long enough for the test.

And that's exactly how I organize and manage my time. I write it down. Even if all I have to do is wipe down the kitchen counters and brush my hair, I'll write it down and cross everything neatly off my ordered list as it's completed. Because if I don't, I walk into the bathroom for my hairbrush and end up cleaning the bathroom floor, painting a shelf, and making dinner before I realize I haven't actually brushed my hair today and it's full of knots. If I don't come back and check the list between every tiny thing I do, the same thing happens, and I've done twelve other things, but not the ones I was supposed to.

I write lists of everything. Projects I need to finish. Books I need to return to the library. Things I need to talk to someone about. My mom will see a list of things under her name and start to worry, like we have a huge, important conversation coming up. Then I'll read off the list, and it's stuff like, we need to reorder laundry detergent, the cat escaped again so can you ask about the porch door, and I can't quite tell if the zucchini in the garden are ripe yet so maybe you can give me a second opinion?

It's mostly dumb stuff. But if I don't write it down, I forget all about it until the zucchini is rotten on the vine, we're completely out of laundry detergent, and I don't think I've brushed my hair since last weekend.

I kind of got lucky on this one solitary thing. It's tricky, but if I really try, I can manage to get stuff done, which is a whole lot harder for a lot of people with ADHD.

Another thing ADHD tends to cause is daydreaming. I am queen of that. My daydreams come in two varieties. One: ways for me to mess up and people to hate me even more. And two: logical trains of thought.

My brain moves fast. It gets distracted, yes, but it moves fast. At least when I'm less depressed. I'm listening to a lecture about reasons Greek art had such a huge impact on Western culture, and by the time the professor has reached the next point in the argument, I've circled through the Latin roots for the Westernized name of that particular Greek sculpture, the Roman equivalent of that Greek god and his story, and arrived at the next logical point in the lesson on my own.

I believe that insatiable curiosity is one of my natural characteristics. Not ADHD symptoms. Like, actual, real, personality traits. It's weird for me when I can even pick those out through the fog of everything else. But I actually think that if you took all the mental illnesses away I would studying absolutely everything I could lay my hands on, positing new (perhaps not entirely accurate but wildly curious) theories on everything from physics to archeology. I probably will never know.

Fortunately, my daydreams during biochemistry class tend to be about the list of reasons why the chemical structure of water makes it absolutely essential to life on earth, and why there is no way that list could be random, and God had to have spent years perfecting just the qualities of that single molecule in order to make life possible.

Unfortunately, this is also the reason it's been so difficult to convince other people that I actually have this particular disorder. I still have some family members who "just can't see" how a valedictorian could have ADHD. It tends to be very hard for ADHD patients to do well in school, because they have such a hard time concentrating. I wasn't concentrating. I was daydreaming about the lesson material. And then raising my hand to ask a question about something that wouldn't show up until the next chapter and driving my classmates crazy. When I was slightly less anxious about making them annoyed at me. I definitely missed a few bullet points 'cause I was busy thinking about the previous point's impact on last week's information. At least my distractibility got me somewhere that sort of made up for what I missed.

My ADHD makes it even harder for me to have coherent conversations with people I'm already terrified of. My brain moves so fast, and so randomly, that people often get frustrated because I'm taking too long to answer questions. I know it sounds a little backwards.

But my mom asks if I have anything to add to the schedule this week, and I think oh, I have to go feed the neighbor's cat tomorrow. Then, they said they would be back Tuesday. I wonder what time. I wonder if I need to go over on Tuesday. I don't know her phone number. I wonder if Dad has it. Maybe I should ask him and text her and find out. By that time, my mom is asking me again if I have anything to add, and getting annoyed that I didn't answer her the first time. But I was still figuring out the answer to her first question. I hadn't had time to say anything out loud yet, and I'd already offended someone. Talk about adding flame to the fire of social anxiety.

I feel like I need to carry around a pencil and notebook with me everywhere and be constantly scribbling down what I'm thinking and trying to make sense of it but usually it moves way too fast to be actual sentences or even phrases, just sort of random words and ideas that are sort of connected. It's absolutely infuriating. I can't follow it half the time. Add anxiety, and it's moving at the same speed but about horrifying things.

Maybe the most interesting thing about ADHD is its capacity for creating boredom.

I owe at least part of this to being sick and incapacitated all the time. It is SO BORING to be too sick to get up and paint or work or at least go for a walk or something. But when I feel decent enough to do things like write, or draw, I still get annoyed fifteen minutes in and then spend another thirty looking for the next thing to help staunch the boredom.

I spend more time hopping from TV show to book to project than I do actually watching or reading or working on them. It's a good way to end up with half-finished shows and books and projects lying around. In neatly organized, well-hidden piles, of course. Still have OCD too.

I get so frustrated trying to find things to do. I write out a list of all the things I could spend time on today and it barely gets me through a few hours and then I'm stuck. I'm too sick for a job right now. So I count the hours of growing anxiety and resentment until I can hopefully sleep, and spend them searching for things that can hopefully distract me from the boredom for a while. Reading. Painting. Pulling weeds. Cutting carrots for dinner. Anything. Slicing carrots might be better than staring at the wall, but its interest doesn't last long. It's so frustrating.

People with ADHD also tend to find things to be infatuated with. Sometimes those things stick around. Sometimes they fade out and get replaced.

My sister loves anything and everything Marvel, Harry Potter, and a certain K-pop boy band called BTS.

Me? I love Doctor Who, any history before about 1700, and book binding.

Art and Doctor Who will probably always be there. But other things come and go. I was obsessed with any and all things equestrian when I was about eight. I wanted to be a horse-breeder.

For a while, it was a certain book series that I was absolutely obsessed with.

Then it was anything Celtic, especially all things Irish.

And in school, some classes would click, and I would become infatuated with the subject. Others wouldn't.

Math was never really my subject until I took an AP pre-calculus class and it clicked. I could recite theory and jump to complicated conclusions in seconds. Then a year or two later I took a calculus class in college. No problem, right?

It didn't click. I still got half-decent grade in the class, but I could no more rattle off beloved calculus theory than I could horse-breeding facts. Whatever love of horses and math I used to have disappeared long ago.

I'm probably not really the person to be writing about ADHD, since I'm still a little new at understanding it myself.

But what I can tell you is that it affects every person differently, just like depression, just like anxiety. And it can sometimes be just as debilitating or just as prejudiced against.

My **worst enemy** is my own mind.

CHAPTER SEVEN

LIVING WITH YOUR WORST ENEMY 24/7 IS A REALLY WEIRD EXPERIENCE. LIKE, IMAGINE HARRY POTTER AND VOLDEMORT LIVING IN THE SAME HOUSE. IT'D BE NEAR IMPOSSIBLE TO SURVIVE ON EITHER SIDE, AND CERTAINLY NOT VERY RELAXING.

You'd think it'd be really painful. And it is. A ton. But it's also disorienting, and even occasionally pretty hilarious.

My dreams at night range from anxious to terrifying and revolting. It's impossible to control my thoughts much during the day, let alone when my subconscious brain is in control.

Last night I sort of half woke up dreaming that I had fallen down and caught myself with my right hand, and broken about ten bones. It was the pain in my hand that woke me.

When I got up a few hours later, that hand was swollen in exactly the same spot I had hurt in my dream, and I only have about half the range of motion I should. Makes typing a little difficult, but I'm so used to pushing through pain that it barely registers. Must've slammed it on my bedside table or something? Hopefully it's not actually broken.

My brain makes a habit of shooting insults at me. Any excuse is a good excuse, right?

"How clumsy do you have to be to break your hand in your sleep?"

"No doctor would ever believe this story, you'll just end up imprisoned in a psych hospital again."

"It's not really hurt, you're just being dramatic for the attention."

The insults are part of what makes it so hard to live with myself. That enemy isn't the sickness. It's not the doctors who constantly badger me to go back to a therapist. It's not the people who are prejudiced against me. It's not even the ones who have fired me and kicked me out of school and essentially trampled me under their feet because of my illness rather than trying to help. It's myself. I am my own worst enemy.

Nobody else can make me feel so tiny.

Nobody else can throw so many constant insults or wish me dead so fully that I shrink into a minuscule pile of nothing and just cry until I can't cry anymore.

Nothing else could block out every good moment in my own life so that the only bits and pieces I remember are the worst ones.

It's me who tells me how much my friends hate me, not them. It's me who makes me feel so insecure that I would rather teeter on the edge of death in indescribable pain than ask someone for help.

It's me who digs fingernails into my own skin and draws my own blood and makes plans for my own death over and over and over and over again. It's me who makes me so scared that I just hide when I should be having fun.

I know it's the sickness. It's chemicals that are doing things they weren't designed to do. It's not really me. I tell myself that. But then it's me who laughs and tells me that's just what I want to think, it's not true. It's just me.

It's a whole lot like living in an emotionally and physically abusive relationship with myself. The times when I fight against it the hardest are the times when I get hurt the most. I have a lot of silent screaming matches and a lot of fights with knives and worse.

And the thing about fighting with myself? Guess who always loses?

I guess you could say that I always win, too, but it's hard to call it a win when I always come out of it more broken than I went in, and I'm usually pretty broken from the start. I guess that's how war in the real world works, too. Everyone gets hurt, in war. History seems to think there are winners and losers, but everyone loses. Nobody comes out unharmed.

I've learned from my own war that fighting violence with violence and hate with hate never ends well. Lost tempers and screaming matches only make things worse. The only times anyone really wins are when they find a way to fight hate with love. Violence with kindness. Anger with patience. Haughtiness with humility.

Nobody in the world needs my love and patience more than me. So, naturally, it's me who's hardest to love.

I hate myself. Or maybe I hate my sickness? Or maybe my sickness hates me?

I can't really tell them apart, so it doesn't matter, I guess, who hates who more. The war will only end when I find some way to fight the fear and hate and sadness inside of me with calm and peace and love. My brain often can't really feel those emotions, even in the best situation. So finding those things probably means finding the right medications or treatments or SOMETHING to somehow fix my brain.

In the meantime, though, one thing I can, surprisingly, sometimes feel is humor.

My brain is gonna keep shouting insults at me. It has been for the last twenty years. Sometimes I can ignore it. And other times I end up curled up in a corner, soaked in my own blood and tears, with a blade held to my wrist.

But whatever the sickness shouts at me, it is kind of hilarious that I somehow managed to injure myself while asleep in bed. I've been laughing about it all morning, in between trying to shut off the insult cannon. If I ever have grandkids, maybe that's a story they'll laugh about. Hopefully by then I won't be my own worst enemy anymore, and I can laugh with them.

Mental illness makes me a liar.

CHAPTER EIGHT

I LIE A LOT.

Most of the time, I don't think people really want to know the truth. Some of them do. But that doesn't mean I'm okay with them knowing it. And even to the few people I DO want to know the truth, I'm scared of telling it. Because I don't want to hurt them. I don't want to push them away and lose them. Or I'm scared that they'll judge me.

So I just tell lots of lies to lots of people.

"How are you doing?" gets a straight answer from one or two people on the planet.

I lie about my cat all the time. When people ask about her, I usually tell them that she's a service animal. Legally, she's not anything but a cat. I could get her certified as an emotional support animal if I wanted to pay for it. That IS why I have her. To be a service animal requires special training, which really shouldn't be the case, at least how I see it. But most people don't know those details. So I just let them believe she's legally a service animal.

The truth is that my life is a wreck and I just don't want people to know.

Not that they don't already. They can kinda tell from the scars on my wrist and the hyperventilation as I force my way through the crowded halls at church as fast as I can without trampling anyone.

I'm always scared that people hate me, but I'm told that most people think I hate them because I can't meet their eyes, and the most I can manage to their questions are terse three-word responses. Truth is, I don't hate anyone specifically. I'm just terrified of them.

So people obviously know the basics. But I'm still not gonna spill the details unless I actually feel relatively comfortable with someone.

When people ask why I'm not working, I tell them I'm taking a "medical break" from school. Instead of that I got kicked out of college and fired from my last job and I panic way too often to actually work for anyone.

I don't usually bother with band-aids. It's just not worth a little piece of plastic. Unless I put the cut there on purpose. Then I'll cover it up in shame, and if somebody asks about it, my carving knife slipped. Or the cat scratched me.

Yesterday, I had an awful day and spent most of the night crying and screaming at myself for things that aren't actually my fault. That's not the excuse I gave to get out of my usual volunteer job, today, though. My excuse is always a migraine or a cold or stomach flu. Not that I don't get those things all the time. I'm just so used to them that it doesn't make that much difference. They might stop me from doing things twenty percent of the time that I say they do. Usually the truth is that I'm panicking and I can barely breathe and as soon as I run out of the building I'll have to curl up and cry for half an hour until I can see well enough through the tears to drive myself home where I'll hide and panic all night.

I know there's some stigma around migraines and being sickly, too, but somehow I get a lot fewer nervous looks and disappearing people when I say I have a migraine instead of a panic attack.

I still feel guilty about it sometimes. "Honesty is the best policy," and all that. But the actual honest truth is that honesty about mental illness will only ever be the clear best policy when people stop treating me like a criminal or a sinner when I say I have depression.

I do my best to be open about it for the sake of fighting the prejudice. But it causes so many problems, I just can't be honest all the time. People have to earn my full honesty right along with my trust that they won't treat me badly if I tell them the truth. I've learned the hard way that honesty pretty much always brings me a lot more pain than the lies.

Even aside from my sickness, there are a whole lot of social norms I don't fit neatly into. Because of my mental illnesses, I struggle to eat enough most of the time. I spend a surprising amount of time every day trying to decide if I can force myself to eat, and what. I've learned from experience that if I manage a meal or two a day, I gain weight. If I slide down into eating basically nothing when I'm really depressed, I lose weight, obviously, but I get super sick. If I can manage a solid three meals a day, I start to actually lose weight healthily. Even though this is backed up by some solid science, a lot of people still roll their eyes if they hear me mention it. So I try not to.

Some sleep research says that people sleep best when they spend as little time doing pretty much anything but sleeping in their bedrooms as possible. I've always struggled to sleep. I sleep with earplugs and stuff thrown over every single source of light in the room, down to the glow-in-the-dark light switch. After I ran across that research in some article, I decided to try it, and was kind of surprised when I started sleeping better. Another thing people roll their eyes at when I say I can't read my book in my room.

I have a second sense about people. I often get a bad or good feeling about someone during a perfectly average first conversation. And then don't see much to verify it until months or sometimes years later.

I'm extremely sensitive to manipulation, partly naturally, and partly due to experience. I can often spot it in people who are very skilled at it. Then I have to decide if I just avoid that person like crazy or if they're actually hurting someone and I have a responsibility to try to convince somebody that this is happening.

And the list goes on. Add up enough oddities, or, honestly, even one, mentioned casually or overheard, and people start to think I'm delusional. They think I'm fooling myself into thinking I can eat whatever the heck I want and lose weight. Or that somebody else is a creep, or manipulative, because it makes me look better. Better from what, exactly?? I didn't do anything wrong! And believe it or not, I would LOVE to be able to just give up on food entirely. I'm forcing myself to eat most of the time.

People just can't admit that their world view is wrong. We're all guilty of it, me included, to some extent. A closed mind. It's so easy to judge somebody based on something tiny that we think doesn't make sense. Someone can't admit that calories in and calories out doesn't cover it all. Or that I might have sensed something about someone that they didn't. Or that sleeping might be harder for some than it is for them. It's easier to roll their eyes and move on.

So I just pretend that I'm as normal as I can.

Lying isn't a symptom of an illness which makes me terrified that people will judge and hate me for the truth. It's a symptom of living in a society that marginalizes and stigmatizes for being sick.

It's a combination of anxiety and social pressure that makes me choose to lie. And it's one of my strongest defense mechanisms, right up there with klonopin and hiding in the dark. So even though I feel bad about it, I'll keep doing it until either my sickness or society changes . . . Or maybe both.

Society IS changing. For thousands of years, humans have been believing in what we can see and understand, and either ignoring or creating fantasies about everything else.

Ironically, we've actually gotten better at ignoring the unseen as our range of knowledge has expanded. We used to believe the earth was flat. Why? Looks flat to me. People used to go see a witch doctor when they were sick. They believed those solutions would work. Sometimes the solutions worked because the people believed. A few of the solutions might have even done something all on their own.

Today, we've got it figured out. Theoretically. We can treat pretty much any illness and cure a much higher percentage of them than we could a hundred years ago. We even have scientists that can explain why the cures work. The demand for alchemical potions has kind of declined, and now the majority of people don't believe in centuries-old cures like crystal healing and acupuncture.

But truth is truth whether science can prove it or not.

Hard for many of us to believe, I know. The universe doesn't actually change to fit our understanding every time we discover something new about it. Energy is energy whether we have the tools to detect it or not. Atoms existed millions of years before we started calling earth home, let alone developed the technology to see them.

I will be sick whether I tell people the truth or not. But my neighbors might do a better job of pretending they don't really know what's going on if I lie about why I have the cat . . . Clearly, society has not changed enough to accept my invisible illness . . . Yet?

I do my best to tell people the truth anyway. I'm not saying I don't lie about it, I do. All the time. But I also fight hard to tell people what's actually happening. I didn't used to. As I've been through more and more at the hand of a society that just doesn't get mental illness, even though it's saturated with it, I have fought harder and harder to change the prejudice that's everywhere.

The first step toward a society that doesn't belittle those with mental illness is honesty. Telling the truth about something traumatizing and terrifying and horrifically painful.

It takes a lot of guts. It certainly gets me in trouble sometimes. I know that it hurts some of the people I love. It can be hard and even embarrassing for them to see my pain splashed across their Facebook feed. It shouldn't be embarrassing. I'm not doing anything wrong by sharing. I feel it, too, though.

It's tons easier to tell the truth to complete strangers. I don't necessarily have to speak to them ever again. I can't possibly disappoint them, they don't care about me. I can look the Walmart pharmacist in the eye and tell her exactly what my problem is and only feel a little twinge of shame for it. Unlike the people close to me.

I also know that my honesty sometimes helps people.

A couple months ago, after actively trying to share on Facebook instead of just pretending breakdowns at midnight never happened, one of those people I love, who I was afraid of hurting, thanked me. For telling the truth. It's still terrifying. But that made it just a little easier when I go to do the same now.

I have friends and family members who will come to me with questions about mental illness or treatments. I'm far from knowing all the answers. I've ended up without a degree or even a job. But at least my honesty about my own experience provides some sort of resource for a few people.

The most important thing is, I hope, that all the others out there who are telling lies to hide their own problems don't feel quite as alone when they hear my truth. My family. My friends. Neighbors. Maybe the Walmart pharmacist, who knows?

And those who don't realize how surrounded by mental illness they are. I hope that my honesty will help them understand and move forward with a little less prejudice.

It's a battle that won't be won any time soon. The mental illness. The prejudice. The lies. This is the only way I know how to fight it.

I can't keep pretending I'm okay.

CHAPTER NINE

A LOT OF SURVIVING WITH MENTAL ILLNESS IS LEARNING TO SAFEGUARD THE LITTLE ENERGY I HAVE FOR THE MOST IMPORTANT THINGS.

So you'd think I'd learn to stop spending so much of what I call life on pretending to be okay when I'm very much not. I don't think it really fools anyone anyway . . . But letting go is terrifying. The thought of someone else seeing my pain is one of the things that scares me most out of the majority of the contents of life that petrify me. So I keep pretending.

This book is about letting go. Not for me. I might become a hermit after it's published. I dunno if I can face the world if the world knows all my darkest secrets. I dunno if I can face my family and friends if they know all the painful truths I'm spilling. These pages aren't for me. They're for everyone like me.

It's really hard just to put all this on paper. I keep glancing over my shoulder scared that someone can see what I'm writing, even though it's just me and three cats in this house, and they can't read. I think.

Apparently, my instincts believe that hiding my pain is at the top of the survival list, because no matter how hard I try, it's almost impossible to stop hiding things. Why? Maybe because the weakest member of the pack gets eaten first. The one who falls behind with a limp ends up dead. The one with sadness behind her eyes has no one to turn to.

When my mom gets up in the morning, the first thing she does is pull open all the blinds and curtains in the house. The three cats who live here immediately claim soft spots in the rays of the bright morning sun.

People love the long summer days with extra hours of sunlight. They vacation in the spots next to the equator with the fewest clouds. They build houses with glass walls to let in light all day long.

I'm an artist. I've been trained to use light to my advantage. Just the right contrast in just the right place for just the right effect. I can use tiny variations of light and shade to build a path for your eyes to follow, to draw you in or push you out, to create excitement or fear, melancholy or peace, to invite you to keep looking, or warn you to run away.

So I know that the first place people look is the brightest spot they can see. Next they see the details in the medium light. But choose to paint details in the dark, and the only people who will see them are the few who study the whole painting carefully, who actively choose to look away from the light.

Most people simply don't like the dark. It's an instinct that goes back millennia. People seek out light because it gives shape to the world. It gives life to the things that keep us alive, and warmth in the dark months of the year.

Darkness, when light is gone, instinctively scares us. The human race has hundreds of legends, ancient and modern, from basically every place and culture in the world, in which something terrifying lives in the dark. In the deepest woods where sunlight doesn't reach. In the deep, dark corners of our basements, or closets, or underneath our beds. In caves hidden from the sun, or in the darkest depths of the sea.

The Doctor would say that evil is attracted to darkness because evil likes to hide. But evil only likes to hide because it's afraid of being found out.

It isn't evil that hides. It's fear.

I guess that's why I instinctively spend so much energy trying to keep up that fake smile. Tons of energy. More than I have to spend.

There's a reason I hide in the dark so much. Because when I'm around people, I have to keep up that façade. And it's so incredibly hard. All those fake smiles and choked down tears. But I do my best to paste on the fake smile just like I try my best to throw on some eye shadow and look half decent in the morning.

. . . Actually, that's a lie. I don't even remember the last time I bothered with eye shadow and mascara. I just don't care that much.

But I care enough to try to pretend I'm okay. Why do I do that? Many days it takes all the energy I have just to drag myself out of bed. Why do I spend precious energy on pretending to be okay when I am screaming inside?

Because if I don't, people are quick to judge. When my fake smile slips, I'm standoffish. When I can't muster the strength to make eye contact, I'm rude. When I can't force my way through the social anxiety to join the conversation, I'm stuck-up. And when I just can't hold back the tears any longer and all I can do is run, I'm crazy.

I have lived my whole life behind the carefully constructed façade of not being sick. As I got more and more sick, the image cracked and crumbled, and it got harder and harder to hide behind. Now, most people know. They know I'm sick. And yet I still spend enormous amounts of energy on hiding symptoms.

Why? Because when I sleep half the day, I'm lazy, even though I was up until four sobbing. When I miss church because I would have spent it having a panic attack, I'm rebellious, even though I spend those hours crying because I wanted to go so much.

When my grades slip, I'm not working hard enough, even though I work on assignments until I collapse and cry with exhaustion. When I ask for help, I'm needy. When I take my medications, I'm a druggie. When I don't, it's because I don't want to get better. When I see a therapist, I'm so pathetic I have to pay my only friend.

When I break down in public, I'm dramatic, but when I hide from people so they can't see me break down, I'm unsociable.

When people see signs of self-harm, I'm just seeking attention, even though I try and try not to let them see.

When I can't hold a job because I'm just too sick, I'm incompetent.

When I'm suicidal, I'm a liability and a danger to others, even though I'm the one who desperately needs help.

And when people learn that I have mental illnesses, I don't have enough faith, or work ethic, or desire to be cured.

So instead, I tend to stay up late. I like the silence. I like the space. And I like the darkness. Not because I'm evil. Because I'm scared.

Grocery stores scare me. They light up every space in the store so there are essentially no shadows. Basic psychology. Things in the light look more attractive than things in the dark. It helps sell products.

But I hate it. Why? Because those lights shine on me too. There's no place to hide. No place where people can't look at me, and judge me, and hate me, and overwhelm me.

With social anxiety, the moment other people can see me, I start to panic just a little. Or a ton. Or I've already been panicking just anticipating it for three hours. When I hear footsteps on the stairs, I turn off my lights so that nothing can seep under the door and nobody will know I'm there.

Any time I'm with people, I'm just acting. I'm just a painting of myself with light colors smeared clumsily over the truer dark ones. I try to smile and nod and give vague total lies when people ask how I am. I try to look like a normal person. But I'm not.

Sitting in church, or in class, I'm not thinking about what's being taught. Every muscle in my body is tensed as I try to look relaxed and inconspicuous so no one will look at me. When I enter a lecture, I find the seat with the most shadow and my back to the fewest people.

I hate driving at night.

A lot of people do, because it's dark.

Me? I hate it because I feel like my headlights are a beacon screaming for everyone to look at me. My favorite spot to drive is those back country roads with no lights and nobody around to see me. The spots everyone else hates. But when I have to drive on that busy road, I put off turning on my lights as long as I can.

And many nights, I wait with clenched fists for the moment that all my family members are in bed and I have the house to myself, when I frantically rush around flipping off every light, before that sigh of relief when it's just me and my cat and a lamp or two.

Because it sucks everything out of me to pretend to be okay. It's exhausting. As soon as I can breathe that sigh of relief, I collapse. I just can't maintain that much energy all the time. It's like I need twenty pairs of batteries, but I only have one and I'm trying to make it stretch the whole day because I only get the chance to recharge it once, after everyone else disappears.

I wonder, if I ever get better and I can say I don't have social anxiety anymore, will my instincts change to the normal, drawn-to-light thing? Or is my hiding instinct so deeply ingrained in my genes that no amount of meds will ever change it? I mean, I can't say I don't enjoy sunny days. From inside a treehouse where nobody could possibly see me even if there were anybody around, which I carefully checked before I went out in the open. Or from a spot on top of a mountain where it's just me and the trees.

For now, I guess I'll just keep looking for hiding places in every random place I go. Don't be surprised to find me hiding behind the dumpsters. Or in the one grocery aisle that the lights missed a little.

My **greatest fear**

is that I am not **worth**

your love.

CHAPTER TEN

DOES ANYONE OUT THERE HEAR ME?

Can you hear me crying?

Can you see the scars?

And if you do, where are you?

Please, please! Will you help me?

I'm so alone. And so very, very scared. Where is everyone? Do they not hear? Do they not see?

Or do they not care enough to stop and offer a hand?

I've spent countless hours hidden, my face chapped from the salt water, my thigh covered in blood, my hands shaking too much to hold the knife anymore.

I do my best to hide the sobbing, of course I do. I wear lots of clothes to cover the cuts, and lotion to make my face look less red.

But people hear. People see. I do my best but I still end up sobbing in the most awkward places. While speed-walking down the sidewalk, or sitting in the back of an art history lecture, or in the Walmart checkout line. It's either that or pass out from holding my breath so long, trying to hold in the tears. I'm not sure which would draw more attention.

People know. They see that I'm hurting. My roommates hear those tears. The random people around town see those cuts. My few friends know I'm suffering. They know I'm in pain.

The people who love me know, but I do my best to hide it because it hurts so much for them to know.

And here I sit, tears streaming down my face, blood on my hands, contemplating the best way to end my life to end the pain. And hoping beyond hope that someone will reach out and help. Praying frantically, desperately, that somebody will notice me, will just take my hand, so that I don't have to do this alone anymore.

But the people streaming past, they're busy with their own lives. They don't have the time. They don't have the energy. They don't want to get involved in my "drama."

I need a hand to hold. Someone who doesn't mind if I cry on their shoulder. Who cares about me even though I'm so horribly sick. Who won't judge or simper or make dumb suggestions that only make things worse.

People like that are near impossible to find. I know it's a high bar. But anything less does more harm than good and leaves me hating myself more than before.

Tons of people offer their help. Once my roommate mentioned that everyone we know tends to swarm around me, asking how I'm doing, giving hugs, showering me with a mixture of sincere and trite compliments, and offering to help. I was surprised to hear her say it. I hadn't even realized it. It's true, though.

I'm the sick girl.

I tell a mixture of lies and truths about my health. But even when I tell the truth, I try to hide the worst of the pain to protect myself and everyone around me.

I'm writing this book for the same reason I've always told people I have depression or anxiety. I can't stand the thought of anyone else hurting more because I didn't have the guts to show people what mental illness really is. I was waist-deep in the consequences of being open about it before I really thought through the increased pain to me.

Those people honestly want to help, I think. They don't understand, though. They don't see that with social anxiety, a swarm of people asking about the pain I'm barely suppressing is a catalyst for a whole lot of trouble. They don't understand that I can hear the gossip, too. I can see how they treat me like a bomb about to explode. Or a wayward soul that they carefully collude to lead back to the righteous path.

And I need help. I need it a ton.

But out of all those people who offered their help, how many of them actually meant it? And out the few who actually meant it, how many could actually handle it? It's not an easy thing. Which of them love me enough that hearing my pain will hurt them enough that it will only add to my guilt? And out of the very few who might be able to handle it, who can I trust to treat me like a person, not a service project or an unexploded grenade or just simply an illness?

I've thumbed through that mental book of people who might actually be able to help me so many times that it's torn at the spine, covered in blood and tear stains, scribbled over and highlighted and ripped. And dented from being chucked at the wall. A lot.

Asking for help is terrifying. And humiliating. And very, very risky. By the time I've bullied myself into deciding to ask, I'm overwhelmed in all-consuming, towering pain that doesn't even let me breathe. I'm slipping deeper and deeper into thoughts of suicide and I'm numb from the battle with myself. Asking is so hazardous that I'm usually teetering on that precarious edge of nothingness by the time I force myself to do it.

It's a frantic, frenzied choice. Picking someone to ask.

I know I sound desperate and bitter and deranged by that point. That's why I need help.

Yet even by those most painstakingly chosen people I am often brushed off. When I'm on the verge of hurting myself, when I am in the most wretched corner of my own existence, and terrified even to breathe, I am often ignored or taken lightly.

This is not a game! I don't do this for attention! It takes me hours of worry and fear and self-loathing to work up the courage to ask.

A very few people legitimately help. Those few have probably saved my life multiple times. And saved me a whole lot of pain.

Even those, though, I'm asking an awful lot of. To listen to the deepest, darkest concerns that I have and somehow not judge me or panic, themselves. To make room in their lives and concerns for mine. No matter how much or how little I say, I'm always absolutely convinced that I'm an annoyance at best.

I hate the cancel button on my phone. I'm already regretting my message as I push send. In that half second between sending a text and losing my chance to cancel, I lose my nerve.

I'll send and cancel the same text five times in a row before I finally send it and shove my phone away so I don't have time to cancel. I'm a little light-headed by then anyway from the wild hyperventilation, so I barely know what I'm doing.

Of course the person I just texted hates me! Why am I so stupid?! I want to just cry, but the tears won't come. I just made another huge mistake and the person now reading my text thinks that I am lower than the scum of the earth and hates my guts. I'm an idiot. I never do anything right, and I just alienated someone who may have been my friend.

Then I get a response and the whole process starts over again.

Deliberating and debating until finally, desperately typing something and sending, and canceling, and sending, and believing I just made the worst mistake of my life until my phone dings. When the person on the other end is busy, the hours before they text back are merciless, tearing me apart from the inside.

But the worst is when the response I get confirms my beliefs. The words sound annoyed or patronizing, and this whole battle did me more harm than good. All those resources. The energy. The anxiety. The debate. The pain. And I lost the gamble.

Even good people who want to help just don't know how. One friend of mine offered repeatedly, "If you ever need a friend, let me know." So when I was desperate, I asked. I was trying to keep myself alive. I thought he was a safe choice. His responses, while cordial, got more and more annoyed. And the clincher was, he started avoiding me. I ran into him and he walked the other way. I smiled at him and he looked at the ground.

When he offered help, he was willing to give me a smile every once in a while. But he wasn't willing to give the kind of help I needed. Why? What did I do wrong? Why do I ruin every relationship?

Okay, fine! Avoid me. Thanks a lot.

But when my frustration fades, I am left with only the knowledge that I am so pathetic and so needy that I drive away even those who offer their help. There is nothing so self-deprecating as knowing that what I asked was too much and that I ruined a friendship through my own feeble and wretched existence.

It might seem to make sense to just rely on my family. But, ever tried to explain to your mother that the only thing in the world you want is to die?

"What do you want for your birthday?"

"Ummm . . . A pistol would be nice."

I'm already often obsessed with the thought that I'm just a huge burden to everyone who knows me. I already believe that everyone hates me. Especially the ones I care most about.

Am I more terrified of being alone, or of hurting and pushing away the only people who sort of maybe like me?

It's a hard question to answer.

So I just lie my way through, with varying degrees of believability. And then after I'm done, I collapse and have a breakdown on my bedroom floor. I'm ashamed of it, sometimes. But I'm more ashamed of the times when I act like I feel and my life turns into an awkward, pathetic plea for attention. It's a disgusting feeling. Maybe it shouldn't be.

Is living a lie really more honorable than living an unpleasant truth? I don't want to be that person who always needs help. But I often am.

I live in a constant battle over whether to ask for help and from whom and how much to spill and deciding how mad they really are at me.

Thank heaven, I've found one or two friends who fit all of the ridiculous standards. Who care about me. Who understand mental illness because they struggle with their own. Who I can make stupid depression jokes to and not be judged. Who make me the first priority in their lives, just like they are in mine. I've stayed up until four in the morning watching the same chick flick over a thousand miles difference just to make sure they're not alone. And they've done the same for me.

Those few people I can actually rely on are the foundation of whatever sanity is left in me.

But it was also asking for help that got me kicked out of school. Asking for help has lost me a lot of respect and a lot of friends.

There's a phenomenon that follows me wherever I go. Disappearing people. I work up the courage to ask for help. And all the sudden they're gone. Or, much worse, they help, and I start to trust them. Enough that I start to rely on them. Enough that I rely on them too much. And all the sudden they can't handle it anymore. They shut me out of their life. And I'm left very, very alone, crying on the street corner, staring at the front door behind which I know that person hides, but they won't help anymore.

I've seen a lot of people vanish when I needed them most. People who I thought I could trust. People who I talked to about mental illness before and I thought could handle it. It's the same every time.

I'm very careful about choosing people to spend time with. It's a giant compliment if I say more than three words to somebody. And

I move forward slowly, sort of like testing the waters one toe at a time. I've learned that the hard way, though.

It seems like every time I think I've found someone to rely on, I get worse and worse and suddenly there are voices inside but the door is locked, and they're posting on Facebook but they won't answer their phone when I call.

I've watched it happen in times when I was barely hanging on to life too often to completely trust anyone. Even those friends I think I can rely on, I'm terrified of pushing away.

So I only ask them for help a fraction of the times I need it. And then I soften it so it doesn't look as bad as it is, even when it's taking everything I have just to keep breathing.

I'm starting to learn by experience that there really are one or two I can actually rant to and tell the whole story without fear. But I'm still afraid.

I know it's hard for them. But when I'm soaked in my own tears and desperately texting anyone who might be able to help me, it's hard not to hate those people who walk away when I need help more than anything.

The people whose backs I see in a crisis never earn my respect again.

It's a lot harder, when I'm already suicidal, hating myself, and putting every drop of my energy into asking for help, to watch someone disappear when I need them, and then manage somehow to stay alive when the person I asked for help confirmed my worst fears instead of alleviating them.

Some of my best friends have disappeared that way. People I loved. People I thought loved me. Just gone. My phone number blocked. Their door locked. Gone.

As if I wasn't scared enough of people already.

I wasn't worth it. I wasn't worth the stress or the time. I wasn't worth the love I thought I had.

My worst fear. Not people. Not panicking in front of everyone. Not suicide. I've got a whole lot of anxiety. Fear is kind of my thing. But what I fear most is finding out that I'm not worth it. Letting myself start to trust that maybe this one won't disappear, and then being abandoned to my sickness. Finding out that all the pain and fear and tremulous hope and every bit of energy I could put into being likable just wasn't enough. I wasn't enough to be worth any love.

I've done my best to be the very opposite of those disappearing people. To always offer sincere help. To never walk away. To never let someone who needs me think I don't care. All of this in between my own battles. It's not always easy, especially with social anxiety.

Don't be the person who disappears. If you need a break, explain yourself. If you have problems with someone, try to work it out. Even when abuse or manipulation figure in, you never have the right to just walk away and leave someone. To let them wonder if you're ever coming back. To make them decide on their own that you must hate them. And, yes, I have a little bit of experience, if not much.

We have a responsibility to each other. All of us. Everywhere. Everyone. No matter what.

So talk it out. Work it out. Protect yourself, if you need to, fine. But never, ever just leave. Never, ever stop offering help where it's needed. If we just learn to do this, we would save so many lives and stop so much pain.

Sorry

so sorry   forgive me,

Sorry!

i'm sorry

my fault   so sooo s

y!!   really, really sorry!.!

Please

I'm so, so sorry!

CHAPTER ELEVEN

THE MOST COMMON WORDS I SAY ARE PROBABLY "I'M SORRY."

I text one of the two people in the world I can ask for help. I'm sorry. I tell them what my day's been like. I'm sorry I always do this. I'm sorry I complain. My head feels like it's about to split in two, but I'm sorry my pain is an inconvenience to you.

I can't focus my eyes the day after ECT. I can hardly breathe. My heart is pounding. I have to try another medication. I can't walk straight. I can't turn my head without crying out in pain. I can't make it to church. My hands are shaking too much to take notes in class. Dinner is twenty minutes late because I'm trying not to puke as I make it. I get thrown out of school three weeks before a bachelor's degree because I tried to kill myself.

And I apologize.

Many people think I'm right to apologize to them. They think the sickness is all in my head. It's my own fault. I should just woman up and deal with it.

Some of the time, I'm one of them. People hate me; of course they do. I'm worth nothing. I don't even deserve a life. I'm just useless. A painful aggravation to every person around me. And so when I'm not thinking about stabbing myself, I keep repeating those words. I'm sorry. I'm so, so sorry. Sorry that anyone even has to come into contact with my sorry excuse for a human being.

Logically, I know I'm wrong. I've lived with mental illness long enough to know that 86% of my feelings don't make sense. And I'm slowly getting to the point where I feel less guilt for being sick.

I shouldn't apologize.

Yes, I am incredibly sick. So sick that I can't think straight. Half the time I can't walk straight. My hands shake constantly. I'm normally having some sort of panic attack.

And I ask for help. Only to just a very, very few who I think I can trust. I talk about the enormous pain I'm in. And while I may hate myself for asking and complaining, I shouldn't apologize.

Because my illness is not my fault. I didn't ask for this. It began when I was tiny, not much more than a baby. At least that I remember. And I fight it. Some people can't believe that I'm trying. But the number of medications and therapists and crazy cures off the internet I have tried is enormous. Unfortunately, no matter how much I've fought and no matter how many times I've apologized, I'm not okay yet.

And I feel so awful about talking about my sickness so much.

But really, YOU try living in constant pain and tell me what else even crosses your mind.

When someone's drowning, they're not thinking about what's for lunch tomorrow. They're thinking about the water filling their lungs. And I am, too. But I'm also thinking about how sorry I am for whoever has to find my body.

People get sick of dealing with me because I talk about the pain so much. And even when I'm not talking about it, I'm feeling it, and it shows in everything I do.

And so I keep apologizing. The claws of that anxiety, dug deep into my mind and heart, keep telling me how much I'm hurting everyone around me. So I say that I'm sorry. And feel slightly relieved for twenty seconds before the anxiety and self-hatred swallow me again.

Honestly, if someone shot me, I'd probably spend my last few seconds apologizing for the blood on their carpet. Or for offending them enough to make them want to shoot me.

I have a (very) few friends who I feel (vaguely) comfortable talking to about my mental illnesses. I don't live near any of them at the moment. So I end up texting them a lot. Asking for help. Discussing symptoms and making dumb jokes about therapists. Or just talking about the show I'm watching and the mice my cat is currently trying super hard to catch through the screen door.

It's hard to talk about normal things to the 99% of people who don't understand the enormous pain I'm in all the time. The hurt and misunderstanding are there like an invisible wall. Even if they're just asking me how to drive a screw, it's like there's a reservoir that they just can't see, and it separates me from everyone.

With the couple of people who actually do understand, it's like the wall is lifted. I can talk about shoes. I can talk about anxiety. It doesn't matter.

I've tried dozens of things that are supposed to help people with my illnesses. But I'll admit that there are two things that score in a different universe than all the others put together, as far as actually working. And number one is having someone to turn to when I feel awful (like, every day). But with severe mental health problems, finding even one person who I trust, who can handle my level of pain without bailing or going crazy, who cares enough about me to listen, who has the time to help me most days, who won't judge me or call the cops on me (yes, that has happened), and who understands what I'm going through, is nearly impossible.

There are four people in this world who I consider sisters. Two of them are sisters by blood. And two of them are sisters by the pain we've shared, the strength we've lent each other even when we don't have much of our own, and our love for each other.

Two incredible women not related to me who I refer to as "aunt" when talking to my cat. Which I do a lot. While she cocks her head and stares at me and then leans over to lick my nose.

There are many people who help me. My family. The family of church members around me. Each member of my church is assigned other members to tend to and take care of and be friends to their assignees. And each of us returns the same to others so that no person is forgotten or left with unmet needs.

But let's be honest. 99% of the people I know usually hurt as much as they help. Not on purpose. I just have social anxiety and making eye contact with a human being terrifies me more than a raging t-rex ever could.

It's only two or maybe three people on earth who I normally feel safe enough with to tell the whole story to. Who I know that if I reach out to, I won't get hurt in return. I'll feel bad about asking for help. But I won't get lectured or judged or misunderstood or any of the other sixty things that most people do that make me feel like a piece of crap.

The ones who really help are the ones who really understand.

One of those sisters I met at school. One of the few who truly didn't seem to mind rooming with me and the adorable cat. And one of the even fewer who didn't just disappear when we stopped being roommates. She taught me how to sass people and stand up for myself a little.

The other sister I met in high school. She has supported me quietly for years. She stood by me when some of our other friends pulled disappearing acts when I started getting worse in college. I'm still slightly embarrassed that I had to ask her what it meant to be a maid of honor when she asked me to be hers because my social skills are just that bad and I really didn't know for sure. It's her kids who are now the background on my desktop.

I am incredibly grateful for both of those women. I can text them all hours of the day and all sorts of raging, terrified, self-absorbed, agonizing tirades. Or rows of sobbing, angry, confused emojis. But they are the first to hear my good news, too. On the rare occasion that happens. And with no judgment they take care of me. They are my rock.

I hope that they feel the same way about me. I get those texts, too, sometimes. Both of them also have mental illness. The pain and the frustration and the tears, and I do my very best to support them the way they support me. And once in a while I even get those bits of good news.

We have a partnership. No judgment. Just support both ways. And I love them more than anyone. Outside of God, they are my first priority and my first resource. And the occasional others who I feel comfortable talking to are the same way. They help me through their pain. I help them through theirs as best I can, and doing anything and everything I can to help is more important to me than just about anything else.

So it follows that I am incredibly thankful for those very few who I can talk to. I depend on them enormously. But every time I go to start a new sentence on my phone, the first autofill suggestion is "I'm sorry."

My phone knows me too well. It knows that I will apologize, without provocation, more often than I will do anything else.

And I do. I'm sorry that I asked for your help, even though I desperately needed it.

I'm sorry that I'm not feeling well today, because if I share my pain with you, it might make you sad.

I'm sorry that I can't be much help to you today because I'm feeling suicidal and using every atom of my energy just to keep myself alive right now.

I'm sorry that I'm too sick to go to your party.

I'm sorry that you're my friend and you have to put up with me.

I'm sorry that I'm so awkward.

I'm sorry that I had a panic attack when you tried to talk to me yesterday and I ended up sprinting out of the building in heels and hiding behind the dumpsters hyperventilating and digging my nails into the concrete wall.

I'm sorry that I'm one more thing on your list of things to handle today.

I'm sorry that I apologize so much.

I'm sorry that I'm such an awful person and such a bad friend.

The very best of my friends know where I'm coming from, they have mental health problems, too. They tell me that I'm okay, not to be sorry. And I do the same for them. It's a partnership where we both hurt like hell every day, and we survive together.

Of course, no matter how many times I read "it's okay, there's nothing to be sorry for," I'm still plenty sorry. Because fear makes you ashamed. I've tried to be a good person. In fact, I've tried obsessively to be a good person. Because I'm terrified that I'm not. I've tried obsessively to be the perfect student, the perfect daughter, the perfect roommate, the perfect sister. Because if I put one toe out of line, or even if I don't, my brain beats me down until I'm reduced to a barely breathing ball, soaked in my own tears and sometimes my own blood.

My obsession with not hurting other people makes actual mistakes unimaginable. And being wrongly punished? That's a whole other story that I don't know if I could actually describe.

I'll keep apologizing, even though I know it's a symptom. Because no matter how right or wrong I actually am, I will be terrified. My own brain will convince me I'm an awful friend and an awful person. And I will be paralyzingly afraid of losing those couple of people who take care of me.

So I'm sorry. For being so sorry.

CHAPTER TWELVE

IT'S KIND OF IRONIC THAT I'M TOO SCARED TO SCREAM OUT LOUD WHEN I'M SCARED.

It's part of social anxiety. I'm terrified but I'm ashamed of being terrified, and I'm scared of people knowing that I'm scared, so I'm too scared to act like I'm scared but I'm also scared of being alone with the fear.

It's almost as confusing as trying to follow the storyline of Doctor Who. Butterfly effect? Oh, nope, that happened in an alternate reality, before he met her and before her dad died and before she accidentally fractured the universe. She's his best friend. Just kidding, now she's stuck in a box for two thousand years and married to someone else. Oops, now she's his mother-in-law.

What it amounts to in the end is I can't ever do anything right so I hate my own guts. It's great. Makes it kinda hard to live with myself. And I'm often too scared to ask for help when I need it, so myself is who I live with. Myself and a cat. Kinda redefines the term "crazy cat lady."

Doesn't matter how well I'm doing in classes or how much I got done today. Doesn't matter how many compliments I get. Doesn't matter how nice my hair looks today or how well that painting turned out, or how many times my cat comes over to stick her little paw on my arm and lick my face.

My brain always believes that everyone hates me. The more important the person, the more they hate me. Obviously.

And the words "I hate you" are probably the second most common ones that go through my head. Close on the tail of "I'm sorry." It's so habitual that it just pops up dozens of times a day. No trigger required.

I've gotten good enough at pretending I don't hear my own thoughts that most of the time I can just ignore it. Takes a ton of energy, though. Energy that starts out at hardly anything. By the time I'm already panicking I can't ignore it anymore.

On the plus side, I have some pretty captivating mental conversations with myself. I should make a movie or something.

Happens plenty when I'm writing these pages. I mean, it's not like I'm not thinking about being super sick a fair amount of time anyway, but trying to make it vaguely coherent to the world at large doesn't really help.

"I hate you."

I roll my eyes and keep writing. "Oh, go away". Rolling my eyes aggravates the migraine pain and just makes me angrier at myself.

"I hate you." The voice is filled with loathing.

"No you don't" I patiently chide, "I didn't do anything wrong."

"Yes I do. Why wouldn't I?"

"Would you please stop saying that? I'm trying to work." I'm starting to feel exasperated.

"Shut up. You don't even know what you're doing."

"Sure I do, that's silly," I'm trying to be patient.

"You sure aren't doing anything useful, are you?"

My logical side is starting to lose her composure. "Yes I am, this is important!"

"You're such an idiot if you believe that."

I try to stop them, but images begin to flash through my mind. This book, someday, sitting on a dusty, dark shelf helping nobody. I haven't cleaned up the crumbs from my breakfast. That's not acceptable.

"You're so messy."

"No I'm not, that's ridiculous. And besides that, who cares? I'm a lot of good things, too," I add.

"Like what? You're not good at anything."

I'm starting to feel a little desperate now. I know where this is going. "It's okay," I soothe, "A few crumbs aren't a big deal. Nobody's even going to notice." But I'm starting to panic.

"You're such an idiot. You can't do anything right."

More images. A conversation with my best friend last night.

"She's probably mad at you."

"Why would she be mad at me? I didn't say anything wrong!"

"She is though. Remember how she brushed you off this morning?"

"Be quiet! I'm so sick of you. She's my best friend." I'm getting frustrated.

"Why would she like you? You're an idiot. You have no social skills."

"Stop it!" I yell. But a nerve has been hit and now I'm thinking about everyone else who doesn't like me.

"He hates you. Why do you mess everything up?" I'm so sure of myself.

"He doesn't hate me. Remember what he said this afternoon?" But I sound weak.

"Yes he does. Why wouldn't he? No person in their right mind would ever be okay with you."

"Shut up!" In my head I'm screaming. "Shut up, you're such an idiot!"

Aaaand . . . There goes my tenuous grip on anything sort of calm for the day. Sleep might reset it. Or something I can really get into, like a VERY good book, or some sort of creative project that takes all my attention.

Otherwise, I just spend the rest of the day beating myself up which usually leads to lots of crying and sometimes cutting, and always getting hardly anything done because I'm too busy screaming at myself about how I'm an awful, useless person.

In some ways, this one symptom is the worst of all the symptoms that comes with mental illness. It's really, really miserable to be terrified every minute that I don't spend just numb, and to try to juggle all the pain and exhaustion and fear. But it's the hate that makes me give up. It's the hate that makes suicide seem like the natural answer. Because who would miss me? It's the hate that leads to despair. Because even if I could get better, what sort of life would there be for a person as awful as me?

It's the hate that makes me shy away from new relationships, because I would only hurt people. It's the hate that makes it seem like I deserve all of this pain, so it would be wrong to fight it.

And it's the hate that no matter what, I just can't fight. There are ways to slow down the panic. Not many. And they're ridiculously painful and scary all on their own. There are ways to break through the numbness. Mostly involving self-inflicted pain, but at least they work for a few seconds. There are sleeping meds that at least put the exhaustion on hold.

But I can't stop hating myself. I can't stop feeling sorry for things that aren't my fault. Even my dreams are full of hate and violence, all toward myself. I have yet to find anything that really makes me feel okay about myself for more than a few minutes.

I can ignore it, some of the time. I have to. If I can't find something distracting enough to replace it in the forefront of my mind, it's a fast fall from there to planning my own death.

So I watch historical documentaries that fill my brain with fascinating questions. Or try to find an art project captivating enough to distract me. But it's just a cover-up. It's like sticking a band-aid on a bullet hole and expecting it to stop the bleeding. It might look a little better from the outside, but the feeling is still there all around the edges of my brain, it's never really gone.

It's easy to turn it outwards, to get angry at all of the things that make me hate myself. But they're not the problem any more than I am.

The hate is a symptom, like all the others. But like all the others, knowing it's a symptom doesn't make it any less convincing when I'm screaming at myself. I still feel it. Just like knowing the pain is a symptom of stomach flu doesn't make it hurt any less, knowing that my hatred is a symptom doesn't make me hate myself less. It just makes me more angry that I can't find a solution, in all the things I've tried.

But anger doesn't last long. I don't have the energy to sustain it. It fizzles out fast into despair which leads back to suicide and hating myself more for thinking suicide is an option.

The hatred is a never-ending cycle. It never goes away. It just takes me 'round the same few options over and over again. Apologizing for nothing, getting angry at the world, then angry at myself, and quickly seeing no options except death. Which leads to hating myself more and starting all over again.

I don't know how to break the cycle. Except for just dying. I've tried and tried to stop it. I hope there's a way.

CHAPTER THIRTEEN

TODAY A NURSE ASKED ME ABOUT MY MIGRAINES.

"Are you seeing someone for that?"

Well, sort of. Yeah, I mean, my head tends to feel like it's going to split open. And there are fireflies. Little gold sparkles spinning around the edges of my vision. I call them fireflies 'cause they may as well be pretty while they're messing with my brain. And, you know, the whole weird flashing neon purple lights and blurriness and dizziness and feeling like I'm about to puke any second. But don't ask me about that, because that whole can of worms just really isn't on the top of my list. I think one of the prescriptions in my collection is supposed to help with it. Maybe?

I'm slightly more concerned about the seventy-five different mental illness symptoms that never go away. Like constant panic attacks. They call them attacks. I think most patients kind of have them once in a while. That's why they're attacks. Sudden onset. Lasts a few minutes. Then it's over and it leaves people out of whack.

My doctors used to ask how long mine lasted, and I was a little confused, so I would be like, "I dunno, uuuhh, maybe four or five hours?" And I would get these incredulous looks.

I know better now. That emergency panic medication that people are supposed to carry in their purse in case one happens? I take it twice a day, because that's as much as I'm safely allowed to.

I had to go to the ER for that a while ago. I was panicking way worse than normal. Normally when that happens I just cry for hours and dig my nails into my thighs and hate myself a lot. But I really couldn't breathe this time. I normally hyperventilate a lot. But I actually couldn't breathe. So they gave me a stronger panic med and sent me home. They didn't even think that maybe I couldn't breathe because I had a neat little list of infections. Influenza, bronchitis, and a sinus infection all at once. They just assumed I run to the emergency room every time I panic because I'm a wimp, and didn't check anything else.

I'm not, though. A wimp, I mean. It takes more strength than most people can even imagine just to keep breathing.

For a lot of my life, staying alive has been the goal that takes up most of my time. Or dying. Depends on the moment. Honestly, they're kind of the same thing. Every minute is another battle. Every breath is another fight. Every item becomes a weapon.

"Could that kill me? Please, can I die now?"

They swirl around me. The hangers in my closet. The pull-string on the blinds. The screws holding together the furniture. A cord. A pillow. A steak knife. A belt. I keep fighting. I try not to look, but they get closer and closer with every breath in. Every heartbeat pounds in my ears, a cruel, desperate reminder of the slim line between life and death.

Sometimes just breathing is all I can manage to do.

"Breathe in. You can do it. Please don't pass out. Just one more breath. Can you breathe in one more time?"

And slowly I move to bigger things.

"Can you move your fingers? Please, just an inch. Just reach toward the glass. Water will help, I promise."

Then a tiny step further. One more centimeter. Another half hour to convince my fingers to close around the glass. Another to inch the glass to my lips. Another to force myself to swallow.

Living with mental illness is miserable, but it's also exhausting. Every tiny thing takes more energy than I think I have, but I have to do them anyway. I can't tell you all the time and tears and pain that go into almost everything I manage to do. Showering. Cooking. Feeding the cat.

Sometimes people (doctors, often) tell me I should try not to do stuff while I'm sick. But I would be an invalid, and lying in bed with nothing to do makes everything worse.

The psychiatric world talks about high and low functioning mental illnesses. People use them to describe whether a mental illness patient has a normal life or not. Someone has high functioning depression because she has a full time job and she's raising three children. Another person has low functioning anxiety because he lives in his parents' basement, his relationship just fell apart, and he can barely even make it to Walmart on a good day.

People tend to categorize how bad a person's mental illness is by how much they can manage to do.

I had a family friend with cancer. I watched her push through the pain as she felt worse and worse. She struggled to come to church and help other people as she drew closer to death, but she did her best.

I have an aunt with rheumatoid arthritis. Her hands are permanently bent in half. I've seen her teach years of elementary school, run her own house, raise her children, and serve other people constantly, regardless of her illness.

Those people, and thousands of others who struggle with debilitating illness, do their best to live good and happy lives. Their illnesses don't make them any less capable of amazing things. Instead, they make the things those people do that much more amazing. And those amazing things certainly don't mean that the illness is any less real or severe.

So why do we think that the things that people with mental illnesses do speaks to the severity of their illness?

I've had severe mental illness for the last 20 years. My whole life.

During those twenty years, I've taught classes at church. I've received art and choir awards, by staying up until one every night working on art assignments and spending countless hours practicing those first soprano lines. All while spending every spare second of my high school career working in the music library, converting teetering piles of choral sheet music into an organized system where you could actually find stuff. I saw tears in the eyes of my incredible choir teacher when she read my name on the list of all-state singers. I've converted tens of thousands of people's names from old historical records to searchable online records so that people can find their own family's histories. I've been the maid of honor at my best friend's wedding and caught the bouquet at my own sister's. I almost got a bachelor's degree with a nearly perfect GPA. And I hope that I have been a help in the lives of a few people who needed me.

I have also spent countless hours lying on my bed crying silently, hoping that nobody would hear while praying that somebody would. I have been forced to stay in psych hospitals, completely against my will. I have barely stopped myself from committing suicide dozens of times, convinced that nobody would even notice. I have seen way too many doctors and tried scores of medications and alternative suggestions. I have spent years' worth of nights clutching my phone praying that someone, anyone, would help. I have hidden in bathroom stalls to hide my tears. I have sat through meetings discreetly scraping my arms to hold the panic in check until I could run. I have staggered the streets of town at three in the morning in the snow, out past curfew, but too confused and scared to be home. I have thrown the things that meant the most to me at the walls in confusion and anger over the crushing pain and terror that have never left my side.

So tell me. Is my pain any less real because of the things I've accomplished while feeling it? Is my fear false because I have fought through it?

Now I've watched my life fall apart after I was suspended from school. I know that between my anxiety, memory problems caused by ECT, and almost constant migraines I'm not really well enough to work now. The sting of suspension and living in my parents' basement as a psych patient is very real. It turns out that now my full-time job is to get better. I'm very much still sick and fighting for my life and sanity every minute of every day.

After twenty years, I'm finally now starting to see a tiny glimmer of hope. Yet now more than at any other time of my life I would be described as low functioning.

Is my hope less real because I can't work and I'm too scared to go to church most weeks?

The past month, I've been fighting this trio of influenza/bronchitis/sinus infection on top of the constant migraines, the constant panic, the constant belief that everyone hates me. There have been days that I've lain on the couch with heat on my back and ice on my head and a throw-up bucket in front of me with Pride and Prejudice running over and over for hours.

I'm exhausted. I know that the only way I will ever get better is if I fight for it. But I'm too tired to fight. All my energy is being spent on breathing and not puking. There's nothing left to go to doctor's appointments and pick up new meds from the pharmacy. I don't have the energy to even fight back the panic that comes every time I think about reapplying to school to finish that last semester. I barely have the energy to get enough food down me to stay alive. There's no way I have the energy to start putting the pieces of my life back together.

But during the last month of lying on the couch in pain, I've also sculpted a lantern. Painted a set of decorative glasses. Cleaned (most of) the house, made cookies, helped one friend and visited with some others, made lots of progress on a book of illustrations, and now I'm sitting here writing.

It's not much, I know. But it's something.

I do my best to work through the pain because it puts what hurts on the back burner for a few minutes. It gives me a little more energy to spend on breathing through the pain later. But no matter how "functioning" I am, my pain and what I accomplish are both very real.

The real question isn't how much I get done. It's: does it get better?

Dang, I hope so. I really hope that eventually I'll have enough energy to pick up the pieces of my life and start again. It's my dream just to have a normal job like a normal person and not be judged everywhere I go for being a crazy, jobless, psych patient. So I keep breathing. Breathe in. Breathe out. Don't pass out. Don't puke. Keep breathing. One inch at a time.

CHAPTER FOURTEEN

ENERGY IS JUST SOMETHING I DON'T HAVE MUCH OF. MENTAL ILLNESS SUCKS ALL THE LIFE OUT OF ME AND THERE'S NOTHING LEFT.

Occasionally on the really, really good days once in a blue moon, when the sun is really bright and I feel almost okay about myself, I'm really energetic and I just find things to create and create and create until everything around me is beautiful . . . I kind of like to think that might be the real me. Full of energy and sass and just craving beauty in everything I see . . . I'm not sure, though. Never really met that girl. I hope I will one day.

At the end of those good days the depression hits hard and fast like running headlong into a concrete wall. And then I collapse in exhaustion. I spent way more energy than I had to spend and all the sudden I find myself in debt up to my chin.

Most days, though, I start out almost as tired as I finish. Everything is a chore. Getting out of bed. Checking my email. Showering. Taking my meds. I spend all the little energy I have by about four in the afternoon. Or noon. When I'm lucky. Just as often, I crawl out of bed wishing I could never leave it again.

Last night I slept about nine hours and got up a little before eleven. Now it's 1:53, I've barely been awake three hours, I managed to eat breakfast and shower, but I'm so exhausted I'm bursting into tears every time I look at the computer screen.

I know I should be writing. But I'm so tired that everything I write today probably won't even make sense tomorrow and I'll delete it all and start over again. And again the next day. And the next.

But I'm sitting here writing anyway, trying to type with one hand and pinching myself with the other to hold in the tears long enough to get something vaguely coherent down in 1s and 0s.

I'm so tired of feeling awful about myself. And I know the less I get done today, the more convinced I'll be that I'm worthless, the more tears I'll cry tonight, the more tired I'll be in the morning, and the harder this will be tomorrow.

I could maybe leave this room and do something else…? But what? I'm too exhausted to do anything useful. And my family is outside that door and I'm already so tired and anxious that just having to walk past someone will turn the terror I'm already feeling into full-on panic and I'll end up running to the nearest place I can hide and crying for the ten hours until everyone has gone to bed and I can venture to put a toe through the door.

And I'm too tired for that.

Constant panic is exhausting. Every minute I spend panicking takes as much energy as a minute spent sprinting away from a giant bear intent on eating me.

One minute wouldn't be that bad, but add all the minutes together and it's like I spend about twelve hours a day running flat out. No intelligent person would willingly do that. It takes too much energy. It's damaging. Good way to end up dangerously dehydrated and passed out on the side of a road somewhere.

I don't really have a choice.

What stops a panic attack?

The answer is that on the rare occasion an answer actually exists, it changes from minute to minute. So it can sometimes take more energy to search for a new way to stop panicking and run into dead end after dead end than just to panic.

And depression? Inexplicable exhaustion is a trademark symptom.

When you feel empty of all emotion, what's left over? A hollow spot where a human soul should be. A lack of all things that give energy and joy. An almost catatonic state of just not caring. I sit and stare at the wall. Ways to die and people who hate me float through without really penetrating. I notice my foot's been asleep for ten minutes and it takes another five to absentmindedly shift off of it.

Sometimes the energy it takes to make my brain work long enough to stand up and swallow my meds and climb into bed is all I can manage in a day.

It's exhausting, being exhausted.

I used to think there'd come a point when I just couldn't get any more exhausted. But I've been proved wrong over and over again. There's always somewhere lower to sink.

I used to just take naps, too. At ten in the morning. Or I'd get up when my alarm went off and stare at my pile of homework for twenty minutes before going back to bed for another three hours.

Then I got too tired to take naps. I just lie on my bed leaking tears and wishing I could sleep. And then give up on getting anything done and take my sleeping meds at three in the afternoon and sleep for fifteen hours straight.

It's impossible to be too tired to sleep. Right? I wish. Being tired is healthy. People need rest and sleep.

The kind of exhaustion that comes from the emptiness of depression or from being so scared it takes every bit of energy to keep breathing, there's nothing healthy about that. It's not like seeing the battery icon on my phone turn red and then keeping it plugged in for a while. It's like looking through all the settings trying to find a battery icon that doesn't exist. So I plug it in just to be safe and it still dies on me. With the charging cord attached. There's no energy. But there's no way to refill it, either. It's just missing. The phone doesn't let me know when it's time to be plugged in. And being full of energy and ready for a few hours of action doesn't exist. Except on very, very rare occasions when I can see a completely different person under all my symptoms.

Sleep doesn't fix it, it just puts off having to deal with it for a few hours. Food doesn't fix it, it just adds to the nausea that the panic and exhaustion already caused.

That kind of exhaustion throws everything out of whack. I don't know when it's time to sleep. I don't know when my body needs food. I can't think straight. I can't feel most emotions. Half the time I don't even realize how awful I feel until I notice some outward sign. Like tears landing on my homework.

Or like when somebody asks me if I'm okay, and I don't even know. I'm just empty. But I can see from the concern in their eyes that something's not right, so I strain to think about it, and I realize that I've done nothing but sit on this couch for three days. I haven't showered. I haven't eaten. I haven't been anywhere. I haven't checked my phone. I guess they're right. I should probably be concerned.

Or I'm up and out, and a grocery store employee says, "Honey, are you okay? You just look so sad." And I start crying and try to fake a smile and run. I didn't realize I was so close to the edge.

Over time, I've trained myself just to keep going when it gets that bad.

When I feel sort of okay, I do everything from hardest to easiest. I clean the showers first because they make me sick and dizzy, then the sinks, and then work my way down to dusting because it's simple. I eat the broccoli first because it's gross and save the steak for last. I tackle the hardest assignment first and get it turned in before I do the easy ones.

I've trained myself to keep living through the pain and exhaustion. But I get so tired and numb that I'm skating through without even thinking, just going through the motions. I'm not even processing what's happening now, let alone planning for the future.

I keep taking notes in class, but when I look at them three days later I can't even read the handwriting.

I make myself eat, but it's ice cream and Nutella because that's what I can stomach.

KBO, as Churchill said. Keep buggering on. Just like I always do.

Until I realize that I'm doing the dusting first and the showers last. Forcing down the steak because I can and skipping the broccoli. Doing the big assignments at the last minute and only getting decent grades on the easiest ones. Yes, I can draw a cube in perspective. Even with shaking hands and on autopilot. The ones that require active thought are a little harder.

The exhaustion makes me think so little that by the time I've scored those bad grades, I haven't even realized I'm just forcing one second at a time. I've stopped thinking about tomorrow, or even an hour from now.

In the meantime, I'm too tired to eat. I'm too tired to sleep. I'm too tired to think. I can try. But I try to eat and end up just staring at my food trying not to puke until I give up and throw it in the trash. I try to sleep and I just feel empty and end up tossing and turning trying to minimize the pain until I decide to turn on a show instead. And then I stare at the Hulu homepage for hours. Or turn something on and zone out so much that I don't even notice when it ends. I'm too tired to come up with any solutions.

Which is probably actually good, because on the rare occasion I can sort of think in that state, it's about how many prescription bottles it would take to fall asleep permanently.

If ever I can get better, I think feeling normal, healthy exhaustion will be one of the weirdest things for me. Right now, I'm so tired of being tired. I don't even know how to sleep anymore. I would love to be tired from a day of work instead of waking up that way.

Maybe someday.

Not all **nightmares end** when you **wake up.**

CHAPTER FIFTEEN

THOUGHTS ARE HARD TO CONTROL AT THE BEST OF TIMES. EVEN IN NORMAL MINDS. OR AT LEAST, SO I HEAR, A NORMAL MIND IS SOMETHING I'VE NEVER HAD.

With mental illness, control is a whole lot harder.

But asleep with mental illness, I can't do a thing about my thoughts. They get pretty nasty.

At night there's not a whole lot I can do.

Unfortunately, my brain isn't sick only when I'm awake. It's just as sick when I'm trying to sleep. Makes sleeping really relaxing.

The unusual amounts of physical pain normal for me aren't even close to the emotional pain that is my life. I can't escape from thinking that the people I love most hate me, even during the day. But nights are worst.

I'm so stressed while I'm asleep that I grind my teeth all night.

My muscles are tight enough in the morning that I have to slowly stretch until I can twist my neck and back far enough to look over my shoulder like a normal person.

Most people have nonsensical dreams about going hiking with their cousin they haven't seen in eight years and having a picnic of curry and cotton candy.

My dreams are mostly about people I love screaming and throwing things at me because they hate me. And me trying to keep up with them doing things while I carry a dozen heavy bags. Always the bags slowing me down while I'm trying to follow.

I'm sure someone would love to deeply analyze my dreams and tell me all those bags represent heavy emotional baggage I'm carrying around, or something.

Trust me, I know I've got emotional problems. Thanks anyway.

So I guess you could call all my dreams nightmares, really, because even the best of them involve a lot of people glaring at me and me making a ton of really awkward mistakes that make everyone hate me even more.

I wish the dreams would go away when I get up in the morning. I start out plenty of days yanking myself out of nightmares and huddling in bed until I can calm my breathing.

My waking life's about as bad as my dreams, though. Believing everyone hates me. Constant pain and fear and shame. Everyone either looking down on me, like I'm some sort of crazy, attention-seeking slacker, or treating me like a service project that may explode if poked the wrong way.

The muscle pain doesn't go away, either. I'm constantly kneading my jaw and hitting my neck muscles with hammers. No. That's not a joke. Yes. It actually helps. Talk about needing a really deep-tissue massage. And the headache. I've had that for about, oh, maybe seven years now. Sometimes it hurts a little less, and I can actually do something productive.

Even the bags are real. I'm a little overweight. But, with social anxiety, everything is giant. I usually carry a coat or bag to hold over my stomach to hide my shape. And if I go somewhere with a coat closet, it does me no good, because I need to be able to make a quick escape the moment I start to panic, and I don't have time to stop off to grab a jacket on my way out.

Also there's the fact that I just worry about everything way more than anyone should, so I plan for every contingency and end up with bags full of everything I could possibly need in an emergency, from pads and pain meds to a book to bury my nose in. At least my purse has Pooh Bear on it, so even if I don't look cute carrying around eighty things, my emergency bag does.

It would be great to have a night of actual, solid, refreshing sleep with no nightmares and no teeth-grinding, and no waking up with pounding headaches. But if I had the choice, I would take all that in a second to get rid of the nightmares during the day.

I'm hoping for, eventually, a life with no panic attacks and no hyperventilating after every social encounter and no migraines or treatments or handfuls of meds every morning and night. A life that's less scary than my nightmares, not more.

CHAPTER SIXTEEN

ONE THING I CAN CLAIM TO BE IS A FAST LEARNER. SOMETIMES I'M NOT SURE IF THAT'S GOOD OR BAD, BUT EITHER WAY I AM.

I zoomed through classes, and by the time I was in middle school, I was reading fantasy books far above my supposed reading level. Hardly ever stuck my nose out of them, if I could help it. My world was always messed up. Hiding in someone else's was easier than dealing with mine.

I knew there was something wrong with me, as a kid. I didn't know what it was. There were a few years I insisted I was a boy…Glad I grew out of that one. I just thought boys were more likely to be the ones hiding out at the top of the mountains hanging out with deer, I guess, and deer have to be more fun than people, 'cause people stink. I think I may have thought that boys were better at dealing with hard stuff, too. I've learned better.

I hated society from the very beginning. I always wanted to build a house a thousand miles away from everyone and just be a weird writer with a dozen cats and a giant library with sliding ladders on the shelves like the one from Beauty and the Beast's castle . . . Actually, that still sounds pretty attractive. As long as it's within range of pizza delivery.

But I also had a weird obsession with pain from the very beginning. My parents would make me put my shoes on to go outside and I would take them off as soon as I was out of sight. I convinced myself that it was just all about being close to nature. But looking back, I remember going out of my way to step on the pointiest rocks and the spikiest wood chips.

I know. Makes me sound like a serial killer in the making.

When I was especially stressed, I would go outside and walk around on the sharp rocks.

I had to do more than grow out of that one. An addiction to pain. That I had to force myself to overcome, not even knowing what it was.

But we're talking about a ten year old girl. A ten year old girl with essentially no friends and an unhealthy attraction to pain. That doesn't happen naturally. I had no idea I was sick. Now I look back and see that that attraction was a little girl's equivalent of cutting.

I grew up to do that, instead. At first, I fully believed that every cut was meant to kill me. I think I was too ashamed to let myself believe anything else. And then I realized there were much better ways of dying, but I still felt the need for the pain.

A lot of people think cutting is a way to get attention. It's not. It's a desperate try at any relief from the pain and numbness that swallows you whole.

Depression is flashes of intense pain in endless nothing. Most of it's just cold emptiness. The sadness and despair that come with it are actually welcome when they peek their heads up. It's almost like watching a home video of myself that lasts weeks and months and years. Everything fades away. Life is too far away to touch, even while going through the same clumsy motions over and over again. I can see what I'm doing, like it's on a TV screen. But I can't feel it.

And anxiety is overwhelming, constant fear that makes it impossible to breathe or think or function but I just have to keep functioning anyway, and I don't even know how I'm doing it.

Combine the two and it's chaos and emptiness and terror and indescribable pain all at once, blending together while never really touching each other.

The physical pain is relief.

It sounds ridiculous from the outside. But the pain is a touch of reality in the vastness of nothing. And the physical pain is a distraction that hurts so much less than the pain of the fear.

I've sometimes gone years between actually taking a knife to myself. But always, when panic is flooding me, I still instinctively dig my fingernails as hard as I can into my skin. And when I'm depressed and can't feel anything, I run them up and down my arms. Or use my finger to flick the soft spot underneath my chin. When tears start coming to my eyes in public, I dig my fingernails into my thighs inside my pockets.

Why? Because I can deal with the physical pain. It's just pain. I can feel it. It's real. I can focus on it. It stops me from crying. It hurts so incredibly less than the fear. So much less than the shame of tears in public. I can hold onto it.

And comparing the pain of a knife to the pain that lives inside me is like comparing the light of the stars to the light of the sun. It's a pittance. Nothing. But it distracts me from the real pain enough to ground me and lets me touch reality when I'm floating in darkness.

I'm less ashamed of self-harm now. I used to hide the scars on my wrist. Always wearing long sleeves. Using ointment that's supposed to heal scars every night. When I was maid of honor at my best friend's wedding, I improvised a special elastic bracelet that I could be sure would stay exactly where it would hide them.

Not anymore, though. I'm not saying that cutting is healthy or good. But I'm not ashamed of it anymore. Well, sort of. I'm still embarrassed, just like I'm still sorry for things that aren't my fault. But I know I shouldn't be. I'm not (theoretically) ashamed of distracting myself from the real pain. It's a symptom like any other.

Unfortunately, sometimes hiding it is much more prudent than not. Self-harm is one good way to get stuck in a psych hospital. It freaks people out and, long story short, brings police knocking on the front door.

Psychiatric hospitals are one of the absolute worst places I can imagine.

In psych hospitals, instead of cell doors, there are no doors at all.

Except on the bathrooms. Which either don't have locks or have locks that every nurse carries the key to.

Privacy is dangerous, apparently. The only way to steal a few minutes of alone time is to take really long showers. But even then, a nurse comes pounding on the door every few minutes to make sure I'm still alive.

The schedule inside there is more demanding than the schedule outside. And the consequences for not following it are more severe.

Get up at eight. Breakfast. Then hours' worth of group therapy sessions and "art" blocks, and free time blocks, all overridden by a list of five different individual doctor's appointments where they ask the same fifteen questions every time. You'd think that asking them once a day would be enough to get the picture, but apparently not.

Patients are expected to follow the schedule, and get marked down for every missed activity or session.

Whoever invented group therapy did not understand social anxiety.

No, talking to twelve other people about my feelings is NOT. GOING. TO. HELP.

And days on end of absolutely no privacy or choice is going to make me MORE anxious, not LESS. But I still get marked up for civilly opening up to complete strangers about things I'm trying not to think about, and marked down for avoiding people who terrify me. I think half the patients make up crap that sounds good to avoid the pain of actually sharing but still get the points. I certainly did.

And then they hand me paper and crayons like I'm three and expect it to make me feel better. It just makes me miss my real paints. The selection of ten ancient paperbacks doesn't help either. Even if I can find one that's sort of distracting, I get marked down for reading it any other time than the tiny free time blocks.

The hospital where I had my first ECT treatments done is one of the biggest in the country, and their psych ward at least has access to the hospital library.

Psych hospitals don't usually offer magazines. Just the pathetic paperbacks. Why? Because it's easier to "accidentally" get papercuts from magazine paper than flimsy, cheap book paper.

To turn on the TV takes special permission to get the remote from behind the bullet-proof glass and locked doors protecting the nurses' desk from the rest of the hospital.

And the food is awful. I mean, I know it's partially tax money, but I'm paying a ton of money to be locked inside this prison, and I have trouble forcing down REAL food. But the nurses record exactly what percentage of the nasty cafeteria food I eat and I get marked down for anything less than eighteen hundred calories a day.

The only tiny ray of hope inside that place is any link to the outside. It depends on the hospital if they let patients keep their phones or not. But even if they do, the charging cable is a deadly weapon. Patients' phones get charged one by one behind the desk. To try to text someone who can help right now is losing even the chance later, as soon as the battery dies. Outside the hospital, when I get really bad, I'm turning it on every ten seconds to see if someone, anyone, cares enough to text me. But even that kills the battery. Inside, every time I push the button is a gamble, losing precious time connected to anyone outside the prison.

And visiting hour. The only time I willingly place myself in the public area, (not that anywhere is actually private) because it's closest to the outside. Trying not to stare at the door and praying desperately that someone will come. And then crying when the last minutes have passed.

Once my friends actually came. I cried even harder when the nurse made them leave at the end of the hour.

I'm not the only patient inside of those hospitals to feel like dirt. It's degrading. It's numbing. It does more harm than good for a lot of patients. It turns us into lab rats. All those marks the nurses make on our sheets. The doctors use them to judge whether we can leave or not. I admitted myself, that first time. I was an idiot. I had no idea what was behind those doors. But even self-admitted patients have absolutely no say in when they leave.

It's less a hospital and more a prison. Somewhere to keep the "dangerous" people who can't technically be convicted of anything. 'Course I'm a good little Christian girl and I've never been to the worst places on earth. Never had to step inside an official prison. But at least there they treat people like criminals outright instead of trying to sugar coat it.

I've watched all the numb depression patients just sit around the edges of the room and all the anxiety patients cower while another patient screams and throws things because they're so sick of being treated like some fanged, radioactive version of a two year old, and the nurses just run interference so nobody actually gets hit by flying objects.

Yes, one or two patients sometimes scream. Or bang their fists against the walls. Or throw their crayons at the floor. What do you expect? You've trapped them in a prison with padded walls. They're missing the people they love on the outside. They're worried about the responsibilities they should be performing. They're angry and hurting and confused and they don't know what to do.

And I've listened as other trapped, suicidal patients like me cry themselves to sleep in the bed next to mine.

If the world is going to become any better for people with mental illness, completely rethinking psych hospitals is one of the first things on the list of changes.

One of my friends and I have what may be a silly dream. If we ever have the money. To create a non-profit organization and build refuges for people like us. People who need somewhere to escape to. People who need a place to hide and cry and not be judged for it. People who need someone who understands to talk to. But who would only suffer from the constriction and shame of psych hospitals.

To build places where people with mental illnesses can come and simply stay as long as they want. Read a book. Cry as much as they need to. Get away from life for a while. Find a friend to talk to, if they want. And leave the next morning. Or the next week. Control their own treatment. Just feel safe and take refuge in knowing that there is no pressure, no judgement, no dumb rules. Just somewhere safe.

For the prejudice about mental illness to stop, this has to happen. The world has to stop treating psych patients like criminals and sinners. And maybe even understand the physical pain thing.

Doctors seem to think that me digging my fingernails into myself is a bigger problem than me having panic attacks every day. I mean, if I could get rid of them both, of course I would, but as long as it's not life-threatening, I see the emotional pain as blocking my view of everything, and the fingernail problem as almost nothing.

The world shouldn't work in a way that makes hiding pain almost a bigger priority than fixing it, and turns psych patients into dangerous prisoners. At least in the public eye.

CHAPTER SEVENTEEN

I CAME ACROSS THIS BIT OF WRITING TODAY. I MUST HAVE WRITTEN IT ON A REALLY AWFUL DAY WHEN I WAS STILL IN SCHOOL, BEFORE I GOT KICKED OUT. I DON'T REMEMBER WRITING IT. I DON'T REMEMBER THAT DAY. THE WRITING'S NOT SUPER CLEAR, EVEN TO ME. I WOULD HAVE BEEN PANICKING AND BARELY CLINGING TO THE EDGE OF STAYING ALIVE WHEN I WROTE IT. BUT I'M NOT GOING TO CHANGE IT. EVEN THE DOCTOR WHO BITS.

I'm scared. And it hurts. A lot. It keeps getting worse and I can't make it stop, it just keeps coming. I want them to know but I'm too scared. I just hate myself more when I talk about it but it hurts to be alone. Which one wins? Totally broke down four separate times today, if "break-down" is defined as actual tears that make it all the way down my face. If I broaden the definition, it was way more than that. I think four may be a record. Usually it's just two or three where I'm teetering on the edge and then one actual big break-down. But nope, four today.

I wonder sometimes if my friends even see it. I feel like a walking zombie, fighting back tears whenever I'm not just plain dead. Do they even see it? Does it annoy them? Am I supposed to bring it up? Or am I supposed to just keep trying to tuck it away where I like to tell myself nobody sees it, which isn't true, I look dead. I'm a decent actor most of the time. The fear and panic and despair and hopelessness and loneliness—I can hide those pretty dang well. It's the emptiness I just can't hide.

I feel like Jamie. The empty child. He was dead. But a freak twist of luck turned him into something completely else. All he could think was "Are you my mummy?" That's all he wanted to know. But he was dangerous. Everyone he touched became like him—a lie that looks almost like life. And then everyone he was around became the same. I feel like that's me. I'm dead, really. I have little reminders that tell me I should be alive, but somehow I'm not, I'm caught between the two worlds. And even though the logic in me knows the answer to that one question, the illness has caught me, like the nanogenes. It's fixated in my mind like some sick, freak obsession, despite all the logic and strategy I can throw at it. I can't even admit the question, not even in 1s and 0s I will probably delete tomorrow, not even where nobody else will see. But I know what it is. It never goes away. I'm afraid I'm becoming the question. Becoming the sickness. Are we even separate? Or is the sickness just me? I'm afraid that if it ever leaves, I won't like what it leaves behind. It will just leave me empty and meritless, no personality, no interests, no virtues. Because it's me. What will be left behind?

Maybe I walked away from what the Lord was trying to give me today. My art class this morning, I left after the first hour because I missed last class and I couldn't do anything else in class, and I felt awful, but I walked out and a girl came out after me, just to ask if I was okay, I guess. And I wasn't. And I started crying. I don't even know this girl. And she asked what was wrong, but I was just too scared. Maybe I was too proud. No. Shame comes with the fear, not pride. Is shame a form of pride? I just basically told her, "I'll be alright." I've said that so dang many times to so many people and it's never true. I never know if I'll be alright. It's hard to know if I will even live until tomorrow. But if I had cancer or something at least I would have a valid reason. Is suicide really a valid reason to die? Do you really make the choice? I think people who commit suicide aren't people who give up on life. They are people who are so desperate to preserve what they have left of themselves that the best option seems to get off the path that is ruining them. They aren't killers, they're survivors, preserving themselves.

And then a few hours later, I was meeting with my partner for a class I taught today and all she did was say "hello" and "how are you" and I started to cry. 'Cause what do I say to that? "I'm miserable and I want to die. How are you? Lovely weather today." She asked what was wrong and again I was just too scared and ashamed and maybe proud and I just choked it back really fast and said "I'm fine" and we just got to work and it never came up again. Was God trying to give me a chance today? I dunno.

It just hurts, that's all I know. It hurts like hell. I never used to use that word. Well now, it's hard not to when I get really bad, because it really, really does. I don't know what to do. Go to bed, I guess. Homework tomorrow. Doctor's appointment. It's just gonna keep hurting. I don't want to have to get up again tomorrow. . . . . Five times. Cool.

Still defining "break-down" as actual tears that make it down my face, five separate times really is a lot for a single day. Normally on a bad day, I'll have two or three mini times during the day, where I cry a little but keep moving, and then after the rest of the world is in bed and I have some privacy, I'll have one that lasts a few hours, at least.

Those full-on nighttime break-downs involve a whole lot more than crying. Wandering around the house opening every cupboard and drawer over and over again looking for something, anything, I don't even know what. Something that might help.

Or wandering around town in the middle of the night in the middle of a snow storm with a sheet of frozen tears covering my face.

Knives and blood.

Pulling everything out of my neatly organized cupboards and strewing things all over every surface in my room.

Cradling my phone debating whether or not to ask for help, and how, and from whom, and then deleting and rewriting the messages time after time after time and ultimately just throwing my phone across the room.

Sitting in front of the toilet praying I can just puke and feel better and never actually doing it.

During most of my adult life, that scene has happened almost every night.

And that question? The question I was too scared to type back then, even where I thought I would most likely delete it the next day? It was years ago now that I wrote those paragraphs. But I know what the question was. Because it never goes away. I still wonder.

Would they miss me?

If I died, would people even notice? The people I think of as friends and family, how long would it take them to realize I was gone? And then, would they be sad? When they got together without me, would they wish I was there? Would they remember me as someone good? Would they just remember me as a problem to be solved? Or would they simply forget?

Logically, I can make a list of people who would notice if I disappeared. Who would remember me, if not always kindly, at least sadly.

But my emotions, broken as always, don't follow logic. They still ask that question. Would anyone miss me? Would they be relieved that I was gone? Who would come to my funeral? Would there be tears? And would they be tears of guilt that they hadn't done more? Or would they be tears of honest mourning?

It's impossible to know.

I know that I'm a burden to people sometimes. That knowledge is not just my sickness. Logic supports it. And I know that I can be pretty self-obsessed. Honestly, though, you try being in enormous pain, even for an afternoon, and tell me who else you're thinking about. It's hard to think about anything but the pain. Mine just happens to be pretty constant.

I hope I can somehow get better. I hope I can move on. Fill up the emptiness with something other than constant pain. Maybe then, I wouldn't have to wonder anymore if people hate me or not, or if they would miss me if I disappeared.

CHAPTER EIGHTEEN

MENTAL ILLNESS CAN BE CRIPPLING. JUST AS CRIPPLING AS ANY OTHER DISEASE. UNLIKE DISEASES THAT REQUIRE MOSTLY PHYSICAL ABILITIES TO COPE WITH, MENTAL ILLNESS TAKES MOSTLY EMOTIONAL ONES. IT DOESN'T JUST MAKE IT HARD TO GET OUT OF BED IN THE MORNING. IT MAKES IT HARD TO LOVE. HARD TO TRUST. HARD TO FEEL MUCH OF ANYTHING SOMETIMES. AND DEFINITELY AS HARD TO FUNCTION AS ANY OTHER DISABILITY.

The last job I worked at only lasted a couple weeks. It was right before I got kicked out of school. I was so depressed I could barely get out of bed. It was my last semester before student teaching. I was struggling with classes. I wasn't sure I had enough money to get through the semester. The times my brain was thawed enough to think, suicide was all I thought about. Seemed like the only logical option.

I've been through a lot of tough spots. My life is a tough spot. A big mixture of fear, hate, numbness, and despair. But those last few months I spent at school, and the few months after my suspension were the hardest time of my life. I honestly believed I wasn't going to make it. I thought I would die before I finished my classes.

But I did my best.

I kept up my grades. My advisor thought I was too sick to pass student teaching. That was one of the hardest conversations of my life. I desperately needed to finish school. I had thousands of dollars in student debt piling on top of me. I didn't know where else to go, I had no other way of making money. And I was drowning. And here I was with near-perfect grades, sitting in front of the man who could find me the student teaching position to finish my education. Desperate. And hearing that despite my A's they wouldn't give me a position unless I could get better. Something I had been trying and failing at for years.

He was right, of course. I would've burst into tears in front of a classroom of high-schoolers on my first day. Grades and social capability clearly are not the same thing.

But I decided to keep pushing forward. I didn't know what else to do.

Maybe "decided" isn't the best word. I couldn't think straight. I couldn't deliberate and make a logical choice. I could barely see one little thing in front of me, let alone the big picture. I just kept doing what I've always done. Kept moving forward, even though I wasn't really going anywhere.

Depression just makes you want to hide and sleep and cry. I don't know how to describe the level of despair that swallows you. The world is just black. Coal black and blood red.

In that state, getting out the door and to the nearest grocery store can be the achievement of the month. Like, really, somebody should give me a medal, 'cause I fought SO hard to get out of bed, and just as hard for every step after that.

Then there're the people. Panic attacks in the pasta aisle really, really, stink.

The worst social situations, though, are the ones that should be the best. I often start panicking when one of my siblings walks in the room. And parties are unimaginably dismal.

Doesn't make much sense, does it?

In general, I try not to think too hard. Thinking kinda tends to lead to hating myself and just wishing I could curl up and die. It's a dangerous habit. But if you think about this, it starts to make sense.

I panic most about my family because I know they care so much. And that at any minute, one of them might try to talk to me about something important. It's terrifying to know that I could disappoint someone else as much as I disappoint myself.

As soon as someone enters the room, everything I do is a show. If I think I hear them behind me in the kitchen, my back is straighter, my jaw is clenched, and my ears are tuned to every tiny wisp of air moving.

What if my sister looks over my shoulder and sees what I'm doing? It's so personal. I don't want her to read this. Not yet, at least.

Can my dad tell what I'm listening to through my headphones? This song is so emotional. I can't show emotion. Emotion is vulnerability. But if I switch it to something else, I mean, this singer's kind of a creep now, maybe I shouldn't be listening to her music at all.

Every interaction is anxious. I don't want my brother to think I'm not doing well. But I'm not, so I have to hide it. But if he can tell I'm hiding it, he'll think I'm lying to him, and then what? And if I slip up, I might trigger HIS anxiety, and that's the last thing I want to do.

And my mom might ask about things like me finding a job. I might be feeling a little better, but I'm not ready for a job yet, and I already feel horrible about it. I beat myself up tons as it is. Can't everyone else stop making it worse? If she asks I'll either end up angry at her or crying or both and it could easily turn the rest of my day into a panic attack.

I often panic whenever family members are in the house and awake. And even sometimes when I'm alone with open blinds. Anyone could be on the other side of that window. Always glancing over my shoulder and trying to sit up straighter and look like I'm fine.

Which makes me feel really guilty because this is my family I'm talking about, I should be fine. Which of course makes me panic more. It's a vicious, never-ending cycle. The most relaxed I ever feel is when I'm alone in the house with all the curtains closed so there's nobody to try to put on a show for, and nobody to accidentally trigger something.

Church is the same way, but on a bigger scale. It's a tight-knit community. Everyone knows everyone else. It's hard to keep secrets. Every person in that building knows that I'm sick. And every person in that building wants to check that I'm okay and offer their help. Which is exactly what I need them NOT to do.

Most people haven't got a clue how to actually help someone with mental illness. It's so subjective. It's so personal. Everybody feels it differently. And everyone needs different things. But even factoring in everyone's individual needs, I've heard some pretty awful things from people trying to help.

The worst is when people want to play twenty questions. And everyone asks the same questions. It's like forty therapists in a row. Just one therapist is like having someone hold a red hot poker to your face. Being surrounded by them is a nightmare. There's another one every time I turn around.

"I heard you had a bad week. Are you doing any better?"

"So you went to the ER last month? I just heard! What happened? Can I do anything?"

Suggestions are pretty bad, too.

"My cousin's wife had some anxiety when she was a kid, and she says that her parents had her try this drug and it fixed her. You should really look into it."

"I've been thinking about this a lot lately, and I ran across this book that's supposed to be really good."

They only want to help. But ninety five percent of the time it just adds confusion to the already enormous pool of questionable options. If I want suggestions, I'll ask someone. My doctor, usually. One or two of the things that have actually helped me have come from someone's suggestion. Someone with the same problems. After I specifically asked.

If you really, sincerely think you have something that might help, email me, so I don't have to look you in the face and say, "Thanks, I'll look into it," while I'm thinking, "I tried that five years ago and it was a disaster." And don't expect a response. And tell me so. So that I can offer a prayer of relief that someone actually understands that I can barely say hello when my roommate walks through the door. I can appreciate people who care enough to email me a possibility a whole lot more than someone who wants to give me an advertising spiel while I'm finding it hard to breathe.

And then there are the ones with platitudes.

"Don't worry, it'll all work out."

"Smile, science says it makes you feel better."

"Just enjoy the sunshine, it's good for you."

I kind of want to slap some of those. Smiling is NOT GOING TO FREAKING FIX ME! Or the sunshine. And do you know how many times people have told me it'll be okay? I'm pretty sure if that was gonna do squat, it would've happened a loooong time ago.

The people who help most are the ones who wave and smile and treat me like a normal person.

Yes. I'm sick. Get over it. It doesn't mean you have to treat me like a china doll. Or poke me with a ten foot pole. I promise not to murder anybody. If you really want to help, just be my friend. Try messaging me cat memes instead of another supposed solution to try. It'll go a lot further.

And understand that human beings are my worst fear in the world. Yes. That includes you.

I get that it can be difficult to be a friend to someone with severe social anxiety. I have family members who still get offended when I don't act the same way social way everyone else does because they just can't seem to understand that, for me, saying hello is a panic attack waiting to happen. But being my friend basically just means doing everything the same way you normally would, from a distance.

So text me instead of calling. Skip the formalities and get straight to the conversation about something you know I'm interested in. Small talk features in my nightmares.

Doorbell ditch a gift instead of standing on my doorstep talking for half an hour. In-person human interaction almost always does me at least as much harm as it does good.

Make casual invitations, but make it clear there are no strings attached. Keep it to groups of one or two.

Come to me instead of asking me to come to you. It gives me a whole drive less to freak out about what I'm getting myself into, and my cat to back me up, which might sound clingy but she's an emotional support animal for a reason. And for someone who has trouble breathing when the whole "hi, how are you? thing gets going, a fantastic conversation starter/diversion tactic.

I know it's all out of love. My family loves me. The people at church love me. They want to help.

And I love them. Or at least I do when I can feel little bits and pieces of happy emotions through the panic and emptiness that live inside me.

But love comes with so much pressure. Pressure that I can't handle. Pressure that makes me feel worse, not better. If I ever get better, I'll appreciate their love a lot more. Right now, it hurts. And I hate myself for hurting, but I don't know how not to. Right now, the best I can do is wave from a safe(ish) distance. Kind of hard while living in the same house. But I don't know what else to do. Just that it hurts.

If you really care, take the time to figure out what helps most. So many people who live with mental illness struggle to deal with the "help" from well-meaning people. There ARE ways to help. Like, actually help. Not just try and fail. But they're not the ones you think. You have to look and listen to find them.

CHAPTER NINETEEN

I KNOW I SAY MENTAL ILLNESS IS WAR. AND I FIGHT. I FIGHT WITH EVERY DROP OF ENERGY AND EVERY TEAR AND I STILL DRAW NEW PARTS OF ME OUT OF DARK CORNERS I DIDN'T KNOW WERE THERE JUST TO SURVIVE AND KEEP BREATHING.

I fight. But most of the time all I can muster is token resistance in a war that's already lost.

What else am I supposed to do, though? Surrender? To surrender would be to give up on getting out of bed, and give up on eating and showering and all the normal things that make a person somewhat bearable. I might starve to death in my bed. Smelling really bad. But more likely someone would ship me off to a psych hospital where they would force me to eat and treat me like I have a finger on the button of a pocket-size nuclear bomb.

No, I might be fighting a battle that was lost long ago, but it's better than the alternative.

People think suicide is giving up. They're wrong.

When all I can do is force myself to breathe and pray that I can stop crying long enough to swallow a little bit of water, suicide is the opposite of giving up. Suicide is the ultimate act of self-preservation, based on the assumption that whatever is next can't possibly be worse than the pain I'm in right now.

It's a fight not to think about death, but it's a fight not to just go numb, too. So I'm fighting the illness on all sides with every iota of my existence and I'm trying to fight my own self-preservation instinct at the same time.

It's hell. I've felt hell-fire. The burning conviction that I am the lowest of the low of the low. That I'm an utter failure, horrifyingly screwing up even the simplest of instructions. I can't even breathe right. Being a half-decent person is unachievably high on my list. It's a good day when I can just roll out of bed and force down half a bowl of cereal.

I imagine that's what hell feels like. The sure knowledge of failure in the worst way possible. And knowing beyond doubt that there's no way out.

Way to go. Had the chance. Didn't even sort of remotely get it right, and every bit of that despair and self-hatred and longing for the impossible is well-deserved.

Which is what it feels like when I wake up in the morning.

And then it grows every time I roll over in bed without getting out.

And grows when I knock my pencil onto the floor because I'm so dehydrated and starved that my hands shake so hard they move inches when I'm trying to keep them still.

And grows when I have to double check a date for my essay on Post-Impressionism.

And grows when that first tear falls, and when my eyes glaze over in class, and when I jump half a foot into the air when my sister says my name.

So then I take all the numbing meds I can as soon as I have the chance, and slip into dreams that I'm not sure really qualify as nightmares because they look just like my days, but with slightly more luggage. Even though they terrify me. All just in time for me to start over again in the morning.

It's easy to see how fast the despair sets in.

When I'm lucky, there are little snippets of hope in between. Maybe I'm not quite as awful a person as I think I am . . . maybe.

I think I'm a natural optimist. Not when I'm like this. When I'm actually me. Someone I've never actually had the chance to know in my twenty six years. But that I've sort of glimpsed in between the fog and the branches and the barbed wire and the gaping jaws of hell now and then. Honestly, I think being an optimist has probably kept me alive. Anxiety keeps me jumping from terror to terror. Depression keeps me convinced that I can't do anything about them, no matter how unlikely they are. I think the optimism whispers in the back of my head that something might change. There just might the smallest, tiniest chance to win the war.

But most of the time? Most of the time that war is long since lost and I just keep fighting it because what the heck else am I supposed to do?

It's on those stupid symptom questionnaires they hand out before every psychiatric appointment. "Feelings of despair, or like nothing will ever get better. 1:0-2 days a week. 3:3-5 days a week. 5: almost every day." Like it's from a textbook.

But it can't be described in a textbook. It can't be described in these pages. I've felt it. I've seen it staring back at me from the mirror. And in the eyes of friends who are as sick as I am.

We tend to stick together, those friends and I. I've stayed up all night just to be there, on the other end of the phone. I've excused myself from important conversations because I know that the little bit of support I can offer to someone else can lessen their pain just that tiny bit. Because I know that feeling. And I would do just about anything to see it shrink a little in the eyes of my friends.

Eyes full of pain but too hopeless to cry. Hands dirty with blood and tears but too tired to bother washing them. Lives strangled and twisted with so much anguish and terror and exhaustion that everything loses its meaning. Laundry. Eating. Shopping. Friends. Sleeping. Taking medications.

I'm too tired to sleep, so instead I sit on the couch and stare at the wall and do nothing to stop the tears or the mucus that just run down my face onto my clothes, onto my blanket, onto the couch.

From those depths, treatment seems pointless.

There's a lot of stigma around getting help for mental illness. Pile that stigma on top of the despair that just swallows life and everything in it, and treatment seems far more trouble than it's worth.

Why go to therapy when obviously nothing can help? Why seek out a doctor when life has no meaning anyway? Why keep taking those meds when the world is black and nothing can change it? Why stand up to take that pain medication for the pounding behind my eyes when I hate everything about myself and my life?

It's near enough impossible to force myself to seek out doctors, to believe there's something medical wrong with me and not just moral, to try to help myself, just through the despair and exhaustion and shame without the enormous stigma that follows mental patients like a shadow.

Turning that stigma around, to where seeing a psychiatrist is as legitimate as seeing a gastroenterologist. That would make an enormous difference in the lives of people who are already struggling just to make it out the door. Fixing that prejudice would save lives. Hundreds of them. Maybe thousands. And far beyond that, it would offer a glimmer of hope in lives like mine, where the war doesn't even seem worth fighting anymore. Hope that maybe the war can change direction after all.

To help? Bring me ice cream. Or a card. Or a bouquet of dandelions you picked from my front yard. Show me that maybe someone thinks I'm worth something, even if I don't.

Offer to give me a lift to my psych appointment, just like it was a lift to the grocery store, not something clandestine to be ashamed of. Talk about mental illness like you would talk about any other sickness. Understand that even though I might be terrified of you, even something as tiny as a sincere compliment can make a huge difference in my life.

Treat me like a person, not an illness.

A scared person, yes. Go out of your way to avoid long conversations and large social groups. But still a person. When you talk to me about local news and what your daughter is doing this week instead of ways for me to miraculously get better, I feel like you actually see me as a person not just a problem to be solved.

Maybe then, I can start to see a little flicker of hope. Maybe then I can take the first step toward winning a war that I thought was lost.

CHAPTER TWENTY

YOU DON'T KNOW FEAR UNTIL YOU CATCH YOURSELF SUBCONSCIOUSLY MAKING MEASUREMENTS FOR A NOOSE FOR THE FIRST TIME.

The first few times I thought about killing myself, it freaked me out so much that I would spend hours praying and sobbing, just begging for forgiveness.

Human life is sacred. We are God's crowning creation, made in his image. He created the universe, the intricate patterns of stars and the unique atmospheric and gravitational and temperate conditions of the earth that distinguish it from every other planet the human race knows of. He carefully designed the inner workings of atoms to build cells, to build life, and then spent billions of years guiding evolution until the earth was ready for us, his children and heirs.

I've been taught the story of God's plan for me my whole life. His first laws for humanity are walls protecting the sanctity of the life he created.

So I guess it's not surprising that when I finally realized that what I was feeling was suicidal, I was mortified.

Looking back now, I think I've been hoping to die since I was little. Tiny, really.

When I was around six-ish, cougar tracks were found in the mud of my school playground. They canceled school for a day or two, just to make sure that no kids would get hurt. But the weeks afterward, I spent my recesses sitting against the fence where the tracks had been found and hoping it would come back and eat me. Unfortunately, it never happened. They could have brushed that off as an accident, and I would just have been remembered as stupid enough to sit next to the cougar tracks, not suicidal, which was actually the truth.

I remember just praying to die. I think it was long before the whole cougar thing. I was tiny and hurting and scared. But I didn't recognize even that I was hurting. I had been my whole life, and even though I didn't know it, I was too scared to make the social connections that would have taught me that what I was feeling wasn't actually normal and had a name.

I did know, though, that God loved me. And that I loved him. So I would just pray that a meteor would hit me or something and I could just live with him. I never met my grandpa, and I wanted to. I figured I could go hang out with him in heaven, or wherever he was. That made tons more sense to my little brain than trying to make plans for a life on earth.

After I was finally diagnosed with depression, I would always mark down on those stupid psych questionnaires that I wasn't suicidal at all. I was wrong.

But I thought that suicide was a sin equivalent to murder and I refused to even consider that I felt that way or ever would. In my mind, it was wrong to feel that way, and I was a good Christian girl and I would never go there. At that point I looked down on anyone who felt so horrible that they would even think about sinking to those depths.

I was so, so wrong. And stuck-up.

I'm not sure I can say that I'm grateful for my sickness getting so much worse that I finally found myself on the receiving end of that kind of prejudice. But at least I don't see suicide as a sin anymore.

Not that there aren't people who have full control of their actions and still choose death. And idiots like Shakespeare and the people who buy into his crap thinking that suicide is the ultimate romantic gesture. Or a joke. There's nothing remotely funny about hurting so much that death seems like the only option.

I know the kind of love that makes you want nothing more than to be with someone every minute. But I'm a lot better acquainted with the kind of pain that bulldozes every desire except to slip quietly into oblivion and never have to deal with life again. So I think I have the right to say that the only real antidote to that intensity of pain and fear is that intensity of love. Real love is the only thing to draw me back from that precipice edge. Real love makes you want to live for someone, never to die. Love is the opposite of pain, like faith is the opposite of fear.

So don't make a suicide joke around me without expecting a well-deserved slap across the face.

Unlike Shakespeare characters and victims on murder shows, almost everyone in the real world who commits suicide has at least one mental illness. Suicide is one of the leading causes of death, at least in the United States. And for every successful suicide are many attempts, probably most of which never get acknowledged or recorded.

Suicide is much more common than murder. But it's the murder cases we see on the news. Suicide is almost as large a killer as diseases like Alzheimer's, cancer, and heart disease. But it's awareness for those that draws billions in donations, and inspires events all over the country to help patients and their families.

Why? Why do we not do this for suicide?

Because we're ashamed. Grieving families of murder victims or Alzheimer's patients go out and fight for retribution or cures. Families affected by suicide retreat behind locked doors until people forget the stain on their name.

The US is finally starting to see some campaigns to stop suicide. But those are still tiny in proportion to the size of the problem.

It's time for the world to wake up. Mental illness is real. It can be fatal just like heart disease. It affects the chemicals in the human brain just as much as other diseases affect the chemicals in the rest of the human body. It can't be cured by "positive thinking." It can't be wished away or fixed with a little sunshine and time off of work any more than cancer can.

Suicide is a symptom of that illness like death is a symptom of kidney failure. Not a plea for attention. Not a statement of blame or rebellion. Not a skeleton in the closet. Not a sin. A symptom.

I was kicked out of school for a suicide attempt, like it was a dark stain on my character instead of a medical problem.

I've been on the receiving end of pointed glances during church classes at the mention of "thou shalt not kill."

I've been shunned by people I thought were friends as soon as they glimpsed the word "suicide" on the artwork in this book.

I don't fudge on those questionnaires at the psychiatrist's anymore. Yes, I'm suicidal. I'm sick. And I don't hide it nearly as much as I used to.

But mostly, I don't pray for forgiveness anymore. Not about that, anyway. I do a whole lot of other things wrong. Wanting to die isn't one of them. Because it's a symptom that I don't have control over. Instead I pray that other people will realize what I've realized about suicide and stop condemning me for it. It would make dealing with it a whole lot easier.

CHAPTER TWENTY-ONE

THERE'S A LONG LIST OF SYMPTOMS WHICH I USUALLY BLAME ON MENTAL ILLNESS WHICH DON'T SHOW UP ON THE TEXTBOOK LIST.

Of course I have anxiety, panic attacks, emotional numbness, lethargy, suicidal thoughts, self-harm tendencies, all those things on the questionnaires that the psych office gives you before each appointment.

But I also have a lot of symptoms they don't ask about. Some of them are recognized by the medical world as related to mental health, they're just not at the top of the list. Some of them aren't recognized, but I can tell you that they're more intense when my depression is worse, or more common just after a major panic attack. And some of them I've tried to explain to doctors and they don't believe me. Or they're so confused they send me to a specialist who sends me to a different specialist until there are no specialists left to see and I still don't know what's wrong with me.

I can only really write on the days when I'm feeling best. I could force it. But when I do, I come back to re-read in a few weeks and can see which chapters I wrote feeling worst. They tend to be verging on unintelligible. And super repetitive. And extra bitter. So as I'm sitting in my living room writing, I'm feeling relatively decent. But even on a good day like today, I could fill a couple pages with the things that are throbbing and spinning. I've learned to tune it out a little, but never enough.

I'm really not even sure where to start, but food is something I struggle with every day.

I have never had an eating disorder, thank goodness. But what I do have still affects how I eat. Usually, nothing sounds good. I spend a lot of time late at night walking around the kitchen opening every cupboard and staring at the food trying to find something edible.

Doesn't usually work.

I'll pick something, pull it out of the microwave, and then gag over the kitchen sink for ten minutes after trying to swallow the first bite. And gag at just the thought or the smell of whatever it was for the next week.

And then when I do find something I can force down, it's ice cream and macaroni and cheese. Not super healthy, but calories are calories.

I crave certain things a lot, too. Sometimes, it's the weirdest things. I'll crave a certain flavor of ramen for two weeks straight. Or Arby's bacon cheddar roast beef sandwiches. Pepperoni. Mango flavored jelly bellies. Not the rest of them. Just the mangoes. Beef broth. No roast. No potatoes. Just the broth. Lemon poppy seed muffins. So I find what I'm craving and eat it. Sometimes I'll still be craving it afterwards. Like, pizza pockets literally feature in my dreams for three weeks after I eat them. But just as often, I'll crave every bite until I hit a wall two thirds of the way through my bowl of soup. And then I start coughing it up as I try to swallow.

I've kind of learned that if I'm craving something for more than a few hours, it's because my body needs whatever the heck is in it for some reason. Sometimes I can make substitutions. I'll desperately want poppy seed muffins, almonds, and bananas for a week, (and I hate nuts!) so I'll google what the common factor is and just swallow half a bag of almonds for the phosphorus or whatever it is.

Then again, sometimes I can't substitute. Don't ask me what it is about an Arby's sandwich that's so different from bacon, grated cheddar, and cheap-o sliced roast beef from Walmart thrown on a clearance hamburger bun, but apparently, it's not quite the same. 'Cause I take two bites of one and start gagging, but eat tons of the other and still crave more even though my stomach is bursting.

What I crave most often is salt water. Ramen, canned soup, broth, gravy, anything that's basically savory + liquid, I desperately need most of the time. I go through an oddly large number of bouillon cubes, even though they're only about 5 calories a cube, and I usually need a whole lot more calories than that.

My metabolism is inhumanly slow. It's proven that some people gain weight, or at least can't lose weight, because they're eating too few calories. I gain more weight at 1000 calories a day than at 2200. I have to be eating either a meal or two a week or a solid three meals a day to lose weight. Normally, I'm somewhere in the middle, forcing down maybe a meal or two a day. Which explains why I'm overweight even though I often have trouble eating.

When I don't eat enough, I have awful diarrhea. Just what you wanted to know, I know!

It makes eating even harder because I KNOW I haven't eaten enough the last few days. And I KNOW that about ten minutes after I eat, I'll get super sick for a few hours. Once in a while, I'll throw up. Usually when I eat after having nothing but a bit of broth for a few days.

In a different strain, my body seems weirdly impervious to meds that should help, even while overreacting to something else. I've tried dozens of psychiatric medications. Most of them seem to just bounce off. It's almost nice when one causes a weird side effect, 'cause at least I don't have to double check to make sure I'm actually taking it. Honestly, until a couple months ago when I discovered a new med that actually works, I could miss my meds days in a row and never notice.

Psych meds are largely hit and miss, and a lot of the time it requires finding just the right combination. Even a med that clearly hasn't worked in the past might work if you try it with a certain couple others. Which others? . . . Have fun experimenting with that. It's like trying to break a lock with 10,000 combinations, but it's a couple months for each combo before you know if it's the one or not . . . Also, there are like, five of those locks on the safe. A right combination for each mental illness I happen to have.

And of course, I overanalyze so thoroughly that I seesaw back and forth for months.

Is it helping? Is it not? Should I increase the dose? Should I drop it and try another, or should I just add a new one on top of the old? Thanks, anxiety!

The un-anxious truth probably is that if it works, I shouldn't have to wonder whether it's working or not. Took me a LONG time to figure that one out. I've done gene testing to find out which meds are supposed to work well for my genotype. And taken most of the ones it recommended with absolutely no effect. The definition of depression is emotional numbness. Things just sort of bounce off. But that's emotional. Medications shouldn't be bouncing off anything.

Somehow, I just don't respond to stuff I should. Two Tylenol should kill a headache, yeah? I start noticing a difference around four, but I usually only take three. So far, I think my liver is still working. I'd rather keep it that way.

It often takes me twice the antibiotics or over the counter to take care of something. Twice the recovery time after a cold. But a little response for twice the cure is better than no response at all, and no response is what I've had to almost every supposed cure I've tried. Thank heaven for the odd ones that work.

For years, I've taken a daily prescription count that's bigger than the number most people take in their lives. Plus about the same in supplements. I've found a single panic medication that seems to work a little. And an ADHD stimulant that directly decreases my anxiety as well as my ADHD symptoms. Turns out that's not super uncommon. I still have a long way to go, though. ECT, meds, supplements, alternative theories. Some combination has to work eventually. Right? . . . RIGHT??

Not having a good doctor all the time doesn't help. I've had one or two that I've gotten along great with. And one or two I haven't. I had a nurse practitioner who was the only person covered by my insurance close enough for me to get to who made life a lot harder than it already was. She completely refused to prescribe a whole class of anxiety meds. Which happened to be the only one I've ever found that's worked for me. Because they're addictive. Even though they're certainly not the only class of psych meds that can be addictive. And I'd already been taking that medication for several years at a safe, non-addictive dose with no problems. She still seemed suspicious that I was secretly addicted to it and trying to get her to supply my non-existent habit.

One of the meds I needed, a controlled substance because it was also addictive, could not be refilled by the pharmacy every month and had to be ordered directly by her. I think she refilled it on time once. Once she completely forgot about it, and in desperation I had it refilled by a previous doctor. Every other time it was anywhere from three to eight days late, even though I would repeatedly call the office. Luckily there weren't side effects from missing doses. I just wouldn't function nearly as well for a week between each month.

Low energy is an accepted depression symptom. And an obvious symptom of not eating enough. I spend most of my energy on panicking and making myself get out of bed in the morning, so there's not a ton left over for basically everything else.

People sometimes try to separate emotional, physical, social, and other types of energy. Pretty sure it's all the same. A bad panic attack takes WAY more energy than a ten mile hike. Too bad, 'cause I'd much rather spend it on hiking. Gotta have something left over for breathing and stuff, though. I've been told that's important.

Sometimes the energy it takes to force myself to eat outweighs the energy I'll get from forcing myself to eat, so I just don't bother.

During really bad times, when it takes all the energy I have just to roll over and look at my alarm clock, I just end up spending all day in bed because I don't have the energy to do anything else. I can easily sleep fourteen hours a night when I'm not even doing that badly. It's the worst times when I actually have the most trouble sleeping.

I can't fall asleep naturally. My brain's usually freaking out, and when it's not panicking, it's performing a complicated analysis of the evolutionary processes that led to the unique qualities of marsupials as compared to other mammals, or some other random thing, and I can't shut it up long enough to fall asleep. My sister, with ADHD, thinks sleep is a waste of time. I disagree. Sleep is my best friend. But my ADHD brain still keeps doing who knows what. So I use muscle relaxers every night. The bottle says they're for TMJ. Which basically means I have muscle tension and pain in and around my jaw, and I grind my teeth while I sleep. The muscle relaxers don't actually do much for that, but they do put me to sleep.

The TMJ is pretty bad, too, though.

A few nights ago, my sister ran into my room around four in the morning. Apparently I was screaming. Normally I don't make much noise, just despise myself and sleep at the same time.

Jaw, neck, and shoulder pain is a constant. Those muscles are hard as rock. They pull at my teeth and bones, so those hurt, too. I can feel the tension all the way down to my toes. Literally. I try to stretch every night, but my life is one long panic attack, my muscles just don't do the relaxed thing. I'm constantly popping my back and neck and stretching, but it still hurts.

That could maybe contribute to the migraines. Then again, so could spending time looking at screens. Like to write a book. Or humidity. Or heat. Or changes in atmospheric pressure. Or just plain what the internet calls "stress" which in my case is actually a medical term called anxiety. Migraines are pretty constant, too. There's a line from behind my left ear, up through my left eye, along the top of half of my left eyebrow and then up through the middle of my forehead that often feels like it's going to split. It's hard to focus my eyes a lot of the time. Everything's kind of just blurry, it's like looking at the world through a heat wave. Things just never sit completely still or line up quite as perfectly as they probably should. Things spin. Or they look mostly normal but then everything randomly jerks two inches to the left.

I try to not wear my glasses as much as possible, because one extra layer to focus through makes the migraines worse.

I wear sunglasses outside no matter how overcast it is, and pretty often inside too, because just the living room light hurts my eyes. I think it freaks out the workers in grocery stores a fair bit. I swear I'm not shoplifting, it's just bright in there. And then there are giant neon afterimages of everything, random bright colors every time I close my eyes, and all sorts of weird stuff that I'm honestly not sure is connected to the migraines or the anxiety or just kind of…both.

Then there's the nausea, acid reflux, and just body ache. Everything hurts, all the time. My feet are the worst. Just random, shooting pain, and then gone for thirty seconds. And dizziness. I'm not ever quite sure if the dizziness is from dehydration, or not eating, or actually just a panic symptom, or a migraine symptom. Probably a bit of each. I run into a lot of walls and fall down a lot of stairs. So far, no serious injuries.

I'm always dehydrated. As in, I try to drink at least a gallon of liquid a day, but I'm pretty sure I haven't had enough water in my system since about middle school. Especially when I'm living somewhere humid. There's this thing called heat sensitivity. When it's even a little humid or warm, all my clothes are soaked through with sweat every time I walk from the living room to the kitchen and stand on my tiptoes to grab a water bottle. I sleep with a fan aimed at me, but I still have to wash my sheets constantly. I get dizzy and nauseous just from walking down the driveway to get the mail in 80 degree temperature. I get heat exhaustion ALL the time, from doing basically nothing. It's infuriating. I can't clean the bathroom without making myself sick for the next three days. I have to plan out chores with a couple of days of recovery time afterward.

Though, honestly, I do a lot better living in the several mountainous states I've lived in than in the Midwest. I know that some people have historically had problems living in higher elevations. But I grew up in a higher elevation, and I do tend to be oversensitive to what I shouldn't be, and not sensitive to what I should. It seems like every time I come back to Iowa, no matter what season it is, I get chronically nauseous within a few days. I think it must be related to the elevation somehow.

The dehydration means constantly swollen hands and feet that hurt to touch during the summer. Waking up five times a night to run to the bathroom just to not be able to pee anyway. A perpetual headache. And always the dizziness. At least it explains the cravings for salt water. I save bottles of pickle brine for my worst headaches.

Another thing that bothers me is a weird numbness sensation. Not sure what to call it. I'll be sitting in front of a painting and all the sudden reality's gone. It's a little scary. One minute everything is normal and the next I'm floating and attached to my body by tiny spider threads. My fingers keep moving but I'm not controlling them anymore--I'm too far away. I sort of feel lightheaded and dizzy, but I'm not in my body anymore, so I feel it but the feeling belongs to someone else. And then a couple minutes later, I'm back in my head. No matter how many times it happens, it's still super weird.

A phenomena called Proctalgia fugax is probably the worst pain I've ever felt, which is saying something, considering all my medical problems. Doctors don't actually know what causes it yet. Sometimes it hits me almost every night for weeks. Sometimes I won't get it for months, and then it shows up out of nowhere.

It almost always happens when I'm asleep. I'll sit up at three in the morning drenched in cold sweat, white as a ghost, trying not to puke from the pain. It causes the muscles of the anus to cramp so much that I can barely move. It's literally a ton of pain in the butt. Sometimes it lasts ten minutes, sometimes it lasts two hours, and

I'm in so much pain that I just rock back and forth and cry and pray really hard until it finally goes away.

Also, there's my pathetic immune symptom. Maybe my body is too busy fighting anxiety for anything else? Whatever it is, I get sick a TON. If I don't catch everything that goes around at least once, it's a good season.

The only things I'm technically "allergic" to are a couple of common antibiotics. I saw an allergy specialist and got tested for the thirty most common allergies, or whatever. Nothing. But if I use things too often I develop something the doctor called a sensitivity.

Winters in the Midwest are humid and frigid. They suck the moisture out of everything. It takes a ton of lotion to keep up. One winter in high school, my lips were cracked and bleeding because they were so dry, but apparently I used too much chapstick, because they were also covered in tiny pus-filled blisters for a couple weeks. I, being a genius fourteen-year-old, kept putting on more and more chapstick because I'd been using the same type my whole life, why would I suddenly develop an allergy now?

Now I have to rotate what kinds of lotions and shampoos and chapsticks I use because if I use one too often, I start breaking out. I just keep a few on hand and wash my hair with one brand on Monday and the other on Wednesday. Laundry soap, too. If I change my clothes too often, I start itching everywhere my clothes touch. Makes sweaty summers tricky. Do I want to feel gross and smell bad, or itch everywhere? I've discovered that hypoallergenic laundry soap is miraculous.

At least I'm not allergic to cats.

There are all sorts of weird medical things that have happened to me that just don't make a ton of sense. One or two would be eh, no big deal. But I can't believe all of them are just chance.

Like, when my appendix burst and I had to have it removed, the surgeon came out and said, "By the way, there was a giant malignant tumor inside your appendix, did you know?" Surprise!

A few of those odd symptoms might just be coincidence, but most of them come with the territory. Even the ones that don't make sense. They must. Severe mental illness affects every part of you, not just emotions or thoughts. It affects how you eat, how you breathe, how you sleep, how you fight off infections, and causes a lot of physical pain too. That's not something they tell you when they diagnose you with depression. But it's a very real part.

Every moment is another battle.

CHAPTER TWENTY-TWO

PEOPLE TALK ABOUT FIGHTING ILLNESSES ALL THE TIME. BUT I DON'T THINK MOST EVER THINK ABOUT WHAT FIGHTING MEANS UNTIL THEY HAVE SOMETHING WORSE THAN STOMACH FLU.

Maybe a year ago, I got influenza. Then after a couple weeks it turned into bronchitis, and then a sinus infection. So I had all three together. I went in to see the doctor about four different times, and I got put on three different antibiotics, one of which I turned out to be allergic to. All in all, it lasted about two months.

My head never stopped hurting, and everything else hurt just as badly. The first thing I did when I woke up was take four ibuprofen and four Tylenol together, and then I wished I could take more the rest of the day.

I sort of tried to function, but by the time I would make it to the top of the stairs, I was gasping for air. I fell down them a couple times, too. I was so weak that I pretty much sat on the couch and tried to breathe for about a month.

Of course, I'm used to functioning with pain. An hour or two of not feeling horrible is pretty incredible for me. There's never any guarantee I won't plummet back down that slippery slope at any second . . . Actually, it's more like a sheer cliff face with a drop of three thousand feet and hell-fire at the bottom. But whatever.

If someone offered me a trade, though, I'd take it in a heartbeat. If I could choose whether to have the influenza/bronchitis/sinus infection for the rest of my life, or to keep my list of mental illnesses the rest of my life, there wouldn't even be a choice.

I fought those two months of being sick(er than usual). I climbed those stairs. I made myself eat. I still sat here and wrote. And then deleted most of it. It's hard to produce anything good while feeling awful. Which makes this book a rather unlikely feat for me. Hopefully it turns out okay.

But compared to fighting the anxiety and depression, those two months would have been like a nice sunny walk on a warm afternoon, not a frantic sprint up an icy hill running from the most terrifying monster you can imagine. I got to do them together! I don't recommend it.

Fighting serious mental illness isn't like a spat between six year old friends on the playground. It's like trying to fight off the apocalypse with a plastic fork. It's like being trapped in a plywood hut surrounded by legions of soldiers with atomic bombs in their hip pockets. It's a never-ending war.

I was born into this war. I've never known anything else. If I'm anything, I'm a soldier.

That's the last thing I want to be. I want to be so many other things, but never that. I am, though. I had taught myself to fight by the time I was starting elementary school. The war is often silent and invisible. No matter how many battles I survive, it always seems hopeless. The enemy is everywhere, and the enemy is me. I've learned to live in constant pain and hide the scars. It's beaten me down until I've become so tired and twisted that I'm not sure if victory means living or dying. Or if it even exists.

There's no escape. There's no sick leave. Lol. Can you get sick leave from being sick? There's no time to breathe between battles. It's just injury on top of injury until I'm not sure if I consist of anything but injuries. Every moment is a new battle. Every breath in. Every breath out. Every blink. Every step. I don't know how to keep going, but I don't know how to stop, so I just keep fighting.

On the good days, when I'm strong enough to fight the bigger battles, I can keep up some semblance of life. Like making life decisions. I think those are hard for the healthiest of people. When you're as sick as I am, they tend to be basically impossible.

As the days get worse, the victories I'm fighting for get smaller. Going out with friends. Pretending to be okay. Making it to class. And smaller. A homework assignment. A grocery run. Eating dinner. And smaller. A fake smile. Writing the next sentence. Showering. One chemistry equation. Then the next bite. The next breath. The next word. The next letter. And then just saving my own life. Not reaching for that knife. Unclenching my fist from around it, one finger at a time.

Today I feel well enough to fight the battle to make myself write.

Last night, though, was horrible. Today I'm thinking about maybe going for a walk and wondering what to make for dinner. Even thinking about what I might write about tomorrow. Last night, I was lying on the couch soaked in my tears watching a show about conspiracy theorist Egyptian archaeologists who think the pyramids were built to be giant batteries, and barely even noticing how ridiculous it was.

In the sun this morning, I'm feeling okay enough to write.

Just those few hours ago, though, I could barely fathom surviving the sight of one more pyramid on a television screen through the pain. But the thought of going without some distraction was even worse.

The passing thought of how I could make it just until my sleeping meds kicked in made me cry out loud in pain and clench every muscle in my body like I was about to be slammed into a concrete wall. Let alone how I could possibly survive the two days before my next ECT treatment, which might help me feel a little better.

I've spent years in pain like the pain I felt last night. I've spent years just trying to live through the next breath in. And I've managed, somehow, to get things done and go to school and sort of function while feeling that way almost every second of almost every day. Honestly, I'm not really sure how. I don't have most of those memories. I remember some of it. But there are a whole lot of things that my family say happened that I don't remember at all. And a whole lot of biology and art history that I know I passed classes in but I haven't got a clue about. I've even got the textbooks to prove it.

I've spent a ton of days at the bottom. Just fighting to breathe. Fighting for every inch my fingers move toward the tissue box. Fighting just to relax the arm pressing the blade into my skin, a tiny bit at a time, until finally I can drop it. One hand refuses to let the knife go, and I use the other to pry it off. I'm fighting myself, my own brain, my own body. I've learned to dig the nails of one hand into the right pressure points of the other to control the one that won't listen.

How do I win a war against myself?

Life is made of moments. I only remember some of mine. I know that most of them were incredibly painful. I know that I fought a war for each one. Living with mental illness, more of them are that way than not. Even the best ones cost me.

I hope someday I'll manage to win this war with myself. Don't ask me how. For now, though, all I can do is keep surviving battles and prying up fingers.

CHAPTER TWENTY-THREE

PEOPLE DON'T REALLY UNDERSTAND MY EMPLOYMENT STATUS. NO, I'M NOT WORKING. NO, I'M NOT LOOKING FOR A JOB. NO, I'M NOT A HOMEMAKER. NO, I'M NOT RECEIVING DISABILITY. NOBODY SEEMS TO UNDERSTAND THAT I CAN BE UNEMPLOYED FOR MEDICAL REASONS WITHOUT EITHER TRYING TO FIND A JOB OR BEING LEGALLY DISABLED. PEOPLE KEEP MAKING SUGGESTIONS FOR WHERE I MIGHT FIND WORK. AND I KNOW AT LEAST A COUPLE OF FAMILY MEMBERS WHO THINK I'M JUST BEING LAZY, SITTING HERE WRITING INSTEAD OF GETTING AN ACTUAL JOB.

I already have one, though. Just living with mental illness takes all the energy I have.

It's Monday morning. I have a doctor's appointment on Friday and I'm already panicking about having a scheduled appointment that I have to show up at.

On Friday will I have any energy? How much will my head hurt? Will I be hovering over the toilet trying to decide whether I want to puke or not? Will I be panicking? How long will it have been since I managed to get any food in me? How long since I cried last?

The swollen fingers probably aren't a giant deal. I can still drive. If I'm seeing double, I might need a ride. If I'm panicking so much I can hardly breathe, well . . . let's hope I'm not.

Will I feel capable of going to a doctor's appointment at two on Friday afternoon? I haven't got a clue.

I hope so, 'cause I have to go either way.

I've held jobs and managed classes before. I promise I'm not entirely void of work experience. I also used to attend things like church activities and hang out with my friends once in a while. Then I got worse. And worse. And worse.

The panic attacks got closer together. They got more public. I got more and more suicidal. And I watched more people run away like I was a plague carrier.

Little things went first. Invitations to other people's houses: Nope. I can handle a couple people, but only in my own house where my cat can protect me and I can run and hide if I need to.

Then all those church activities: Too many people. Too much panic.

Next I was missing church every other week: So many people wanting to know, "how are you?"

Skipping less important classes: Still not sure how I managed to pull A's.

Paying an extra couple hundred to not have to share a bedroom: True desperation when you don't have an extra couple dollars, let alone a couple hundred.

It wasn't long before getting suspended that I applied for the lowest of the low fast food jobs in a tiny college town. I was obsessed with death by that point. I was so, so sick. But I couldn't afford that private room on my minimal loans, and being within eyesight of a roommate made my heart race. I had to have a private room to hide in.

I dunno why they hired me, really. There are way more workers than jobs in a little college town like that.

It lasted two weeks. I was so tired. I spent my breaks crying out back. I couldn't keep up. I couldn't cope. I don't remember much of those last few semesters, but I remember the under-manager just shaking his head. That's all he ever gave me, just a sad head shake and a single check. I think he felt bad. It was glaringly obvious something was wrong with me, I'm sure they knew.

Three years later, I can usually walk through the living room without panicking. When I'm already bad, just being in the same room as someone feels like their eyes are burning into me. But, mostly, I'm doing better.

Back then, every day was hell, and I just counted the seconds until I could go back to bed. Now, my days are basically defined by how long I manage to fight off my worst symptoms for. A fair few are still pretty hellish, but at least I can often manage not to panic until evening.

I still can't go to other people's houses. I still can't go to church. Not at all, right now. I can make it to the corner grocery store most days.

But my relationship with calm productivity is still pretty tenuous. Any one of a few dozen factors changes, and all the sudden I'm too sick to handle taking out the trash. Add a calendar date, and the stakes get higher.

Soon. Maybe? I keep telling myself it'll be soon. When I'll be ready. But in actuality, it's gonna start with working up the courage to sit through the first ten minutes of church in the foyer. And then the first twenty. Maybe once I get started, it'll be easier. Right now, though, a normal job with hours and a paycheck is universes away.

Hopefully, I can find other ways of living. More anxiety-friendly ways. Even in writing this book, though, once in a while I feel well enough to write a few days in a row. And sometimes it's three months of berating myself for not writing, but I'm just too sick.

So, no, I can't handle a regular job at the moment. Please just stop asking. Believe me, nobody feels the need to be useful more than I do. But I'm a little bit busy fighting. Just trying to live and feel a little less pain tomorrow than yesterday. When I get to a point where I can manage the pain of every day, then we can talk.

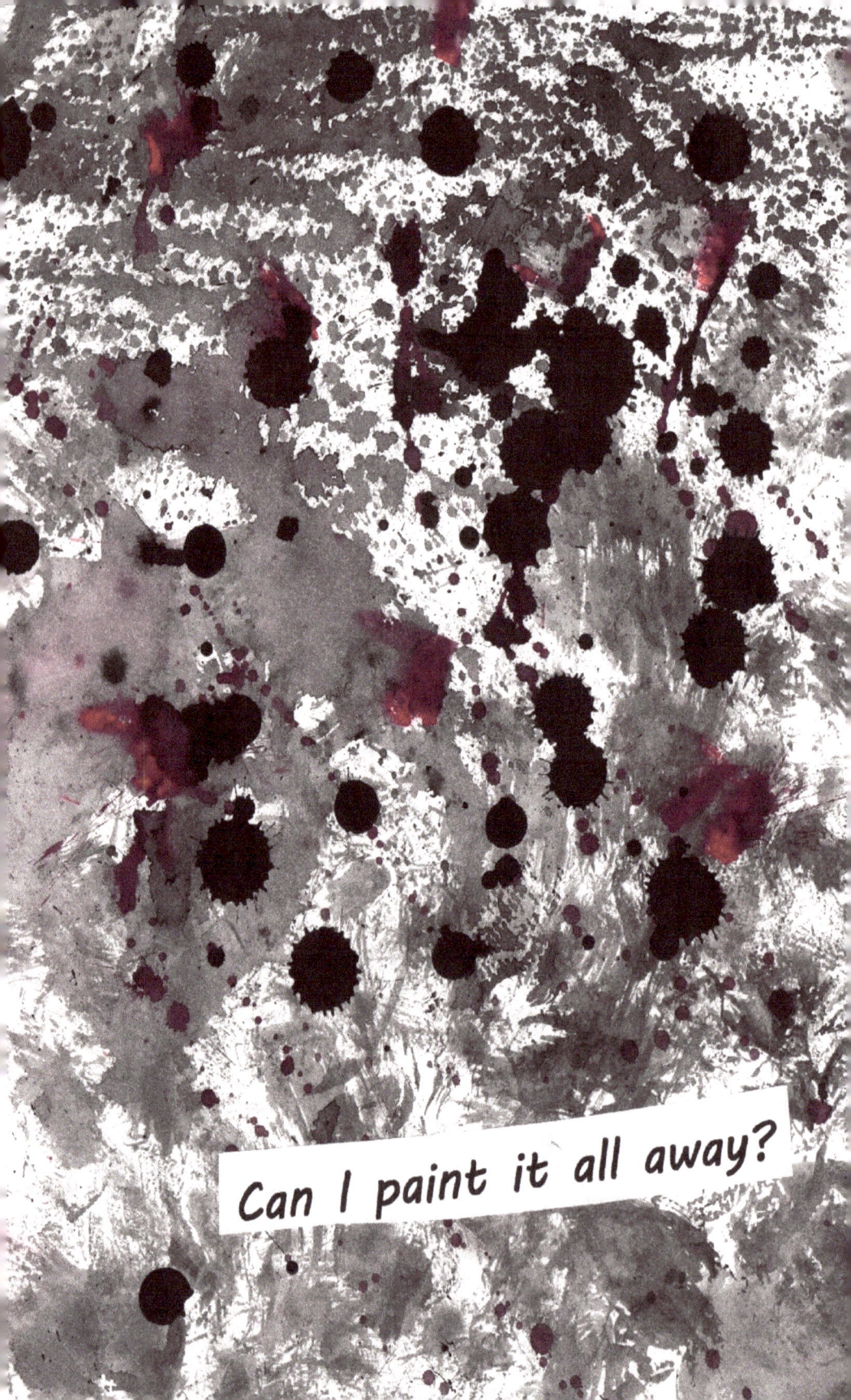

CHAPTER TWENTY-FOUR

THE WORLD LIKES TO THINK THAT CREATIVITY IS FED BY THE CHRONIC SUFFERING OF MENTAL ILLNESS, AND THAT ALL TRULY CREATIVE PEOPLE ARE MENTALLY ILL. THE IDEA COMES FROM THE FEW CREATIVE MASTERS WHO HAVE VERY REAL DOCUMENTED SYMPTOMS OF MENTAL ILLNESS. PEOPLE LIKE VINCENT VAN GOGH, ONE OF THE MOST FAMOUS ARTISTS IN THE WORLD. OR LIKE LUDWIG VAN BEETHOVEN, WHO WROTE SOME OF THE MOST RECOGNIZABLE PIECES OF MUSIC IN HISTORY.

That lie is so ludicrous I'm honestly not sure how it's survived.

Mental illness kills creativity stone cold dead.

I love the rush of energy and excitement that comes with that new idea, and the absorption so total that I can spend eight hours flinging paint around and never notice that the sun's gone down and I've forgotten to eat. Probably the happiest moments of my life have been spent with a paintbrush or a lump of clay in hand.

With severe mental illness, happy moments don't come easy. On the rare occasion I do feel real positive emotion, it's confusing. I don't recognize the feeling, and it takes stepping back and evaluating to realize that there are actually endorphins working in my brain.

I often wonder—if I somehow, someday manage to get better, to really control the set of mental illnesses that seem to have shaped my life for the last twenty years—will I even recognize myself? My whole life, my brain has only been capable of blocking good emotions and creating needless, obsessive, frantic fear.

So if my brain were healed and I could finally feel what normal people feel? Would I know how to function without the fear? Would there be an enormous hole where the disease used to be? Or am I the disease? Maybe nothing would be left.

But then, maybe I would find that there is much more to me than I ever could imagine today. And maybe I would suddenly see much more to the world than was there before. My world of terror, nurses' needles, despair, doctors, marginalization and prejudice, giant handfuls of prescription pills, and pain that never stops, never leaves me time to breathe. Maybe in its place would be a new world of light. Room to think and breathe and imagine.

Today I create to live. In my life of darkness, those moments of seeing something new fall together are a glimmer of light.

Don't be fooled, creating is hard work. It takes long nights of practice and hundreds of failed attempts for every real success. And I can't create when I'm depressed, or panicking, or so exhausted I can't eat and I can't breathe. The cold, barren emptiness. The swirling panic. The overwhelming despair that comes of knowing my own utter worthlessness and leaves me so ravaged I can't hope to move, let alone function in the lowest sense.

So when do I create? Not often.

That doesn't mean I don't draw, or sculpt, or paint. But my work is forced. A textbook still life with no life, just still. An exact figure drawing, perfectly shaded, lacking any individuality or energy. I've turned in many an important homework assignment looking like I drew it half asleep, a fair number with hastily wiped up tear stains, and even a few with painted-over blood. That's not creating.

Creating is the times when I pick up a brush and feel just a little respite. Just a tiny bit of energy in a flat-lined world. A minuscule rush of calm that interrupts the unreasoning terror that surrounds me. Sometimes even enough to move the terror to the back of my mind, just for a few minutes.

Someone reading this book probably can't tell. But I can look at the illustrations and know which ones I actually felt, and which ones just followed the rules.

A lot of my artwork involves mental illness in some way. You can only create on top of what you know, and sickness is mostly what I know. A lot of it's just forced. No tangents. The right objects in the right places. Good proportions. Well-thought-out color schemes.

A few of them, though, actually make sense. At least to me. They make me feel something that's not just fear. Sometimes it's the darkest ones about things that would terrify the average person, and sometimes it's a dumb value scale assignment. It's the few that fell at just the right moment to actually let me feel a desire to create.

Most of the time I don't really want to do much besides die or hide from the world. It has to be just the right opportunity, when my brain is least sick, for something to hold enough allure to filter through all the messed up chemicals and make me actually want to do something. Something that doesn't involve mindless distraction and/or dark empty rooms for hours on end.

And for me, the thing that filters through most often is making things. Sometimes it's inventing a new type of cookie. Doesn't have to be paper and pencil. But almost always, it's creating something.

This is how I live. By creating. Everything else is survival, desperate self-defense in an arctic desert of hurt. Those moments I spend in that fluid world of creativity are the fuel for my survival.

So are artists more likely to have mental illness? That's so backwards it's laughable. The mental processes cancel each other out. Does my mental illness make me a better artist? Most of the time, definitely not. But I hope so. Just every once in a while, when I can sort of feel. I hope--like I hope for that new girl who no longer lives in pain—I hope my creativity can give hope to someone else out there.

And I hope that someday I can live to create, not just create to live.

I would love to have so many ideas that I can't finish one before moving on to the next, like Leonardo da Vinci. He was famous for never completing anything because he had become obsessed with the next idea and started a new project.

I have a habit of leaving half-finished projects lying around, too, but it's not because I've moved on to a new one. It's because all my energy is being spent just trying to get through the pain and I don't have any left over for finishing things.

Creating is a way of life. Mental illness is a way of surviving long enough to take the next breath and hopefully hurting a tiny bit less. They both take up a lot of space. But one is thrilling and satisfying while the other is so painful that life seems pointless.

In the moments I can feel, I want so badly just to live with a paintbrush in hand and forget all of the pain. I can't, though. The chemicals won't let me. I'm trapped in my own brain with layers and layers of five-foot thick walls keeping me in. I can hope, though . . . Actually I can't, it's physically impossible for me. You know what I mean, though. I can keep that vision in the back of my mind and just work for it and maybe someday it'll actually happen.

God is my only friend

CHAPTER TWENTY-FIVE

I LOVE CEMETERIES. IT SOUNDS CREEPY, I KNOW.

Maybe it's partly because I love history. Not the wars and stats. The real, average people. Each headstone symbolizes a real person who had a life, a personality, and people who loved them enough to remember and celebrate their life when it was over.

Then again, maybe it's because cemeteries are some of the most peaceful places on earth. Even in the middle of a city, cemeteries are quiet and green. I have to hide a lot just to survive, but in cemeteries, hiding from the world feels like exploring, not hiding. Every headstone represents a story. Someone who could have been a friend.

Real friends are hard to come by when you're as sick as I am. It's no fun to hang out with the girl who's always crying. Not to mention that being exhausted all the time doesn't leave much energy for anything not strictly necessary to not being a complete failure.

Not that I haven't managed to do that anyway.

I've managed to find a few good friends.

Most of the time, though, I rely most on God.

I was lucky to be raised knowing about God and his love for each person on earth.

Unfortunately, a strong belief in anything is usually rooted in feelings of peace and faith. Mental illness sucks all the positive emotions out of people. Things like peace and joy and faith are just remote concepts that don't mean much.

Depression, especially, is like a vacuum. Everything that I'm made of slips away and the only thing left is a big, jagged hole where I should be. The only things that get through are panic and pain. Any emotional trigger is a bad trigger. A lot of the time I feel nothing, just blackness, but someone starts talking about happiness and I panic the same way I panic when someone starts talking about suicide. Knowing that there's happiness out there that I can't hope to find is as painful as wanting death.

So things like faith and finding peace in God? Not really happening.

The way God usually communicates with people is with emotions. It's awfully hard to believe in a God when all your emotions are bad ones. A lot of people with problems as big as mine end up bitter and angry, not believing in anything or trusting anyone.

It's easy to get that way. Sometimes I wonder why I have to deal with this living hell. It's easy to blame God.

But he created us and everything else to teach us to become like him. If we never learn, things never get any better.

A lot of the time all I feel is numb with bits of terror and despair and hate thrown in. During those times, when I can't really feel things like faith and hope, I have to stick to logic. Logically, I know there is a God. Logically, I know that this earth is too beautiful and seamless to have come from anywhere but the studio of eternity's greatest artist and scientist. Logic tells me that no amount of chance could have created the varied and complex life that supports the human race. Logically, I know that God is there for me, that he lived and died for me, that he loves me. I remember that I believe those things, but no amount of focusing on the memory of belief can make me feel it again.

So even in the darkest times, I keep praying. I keep reading the scriptures. I keep trying to be a good person even when every tiny piece of me is screaming that I am worthless and broken.

And more than anything, it's paid off. I've learned to see tiny miracles in a world of black terror. A momentary flash of peace when I pray. A thank you from someone that reminds me for just a second that maybe I'm actually worth something.

I have one friend who is never busy in class or work, a friend who shows me miracles every day. It's taken me a lot of time and work to find a relationship with God through the pain and numbness. But I've gotten better at recognizing those flashes of calm that come with prayer, the understanding that comes with asking for answers, and the little bits of peace that come with doing what's right.

I've even learned to feel the spirit of God. FEEL it! When I pray and ask questions, or when I catch glimpses of truth through the haze. I feel something that must be joy and peace. Just for a minute.

Those emotions aren't natural for me. My brain is too broken to manufacture them even when they're appropriate. Those pieces of positive emotion that I feel almost always come from him. Every single one is a miracle.

It doesn't make up for the living hell of mental illness. But a lot of the time, God is the only friend I can turn to when I feel my worst. Including at three in the morning when I can't sleep and when the things that trigger panic are so trivial they're embarrassing. I'm thankful for his help in this mess that happens to be my life.

I know that many of you reading this probably don't believe in a God, or aren't sure what you believe, especially with mental illness. Or think that if he exists, he has abandoned you.

This book isn't about making people believe in a God. This book is about helping people believe in the reality of mental illness, and in the power inside of themselves.

So if you don't believe in a God, believe in this. The universe around us, in all its beauty, is the source of everything that makes up humanity. Each of us are made of atoms that come from the world around us.

Amid all the products of the universe are beautiful things, but there are broken things, too. Every person is broken somehow. Sometimes life does the breaking. Sometimes we're just born broken. I was born with the genes that make my brain a factory for every bad emotion you can imagine.

But broken things can be fixed. And sometimes, the product of repairs can be more gorgeous and even more functional than the original.

There is help around you! It doesn't seem like it, I know. But God, or nature, or science, fixes the things that it breaks. And in the end, the best people are the ones who have broken and been patient as they, with the help of the people and world around them, patched their lives back together.

I've learned that sometimes people abandon God, but he never abandons people. No matter how much pain there is, he will always be there to help us learn to be better people through it. Pain doesn't mean he's not there, it just means there's something he needs us to learn or to do in order to become the person he wants us to be.

Each of the people who has ever been on the earth is a child of God, and the same God loves me. Sitting on the grass in a cemetery, surrounded by the reminders of lives lived, I can feel a little bit of that love for every person, and a little understanding through the haze. They're places I can almost feel a little bit of something positive. Where God is a little closer.

Each of us can reach out and take advantage of that. Whether it's God you believe in, or something else. It seems impossibly far away. It seems like nothing or no one could help. But if you reach out and try to find it, it's there. It might take a while to find. It might take even longer to understand. But it IS there. No matter how sick or in how much pain or how numb you are. It's there.

CHAPTER TWENTY-SIX

WE ALL HAVE PREJUDICES ABOUT MENTAL ILLNESS. INCLUDING ME, AND I'VE BEEN DEALING WITH IT MY WHOLE LIFE. PEOPLE WHO WANT TO HELP HAVE THEM, TOO. WEIRDLY, A LOT OF THE TIME, THE PEOPLE WHO OFFER TO HELP HAVE MORE STEREOTYPICAL BELIEFS THAN THE ONES WHO DON'T, AND TREAT ME LIKE I'M A BOMB ABOUT TO GO OFF.

Most of the time, though, as soon as people learn that I'm sick, they just disappear. They know I need help. But they don't know how to deal with it. Or they're too afraid. Or they're just plain too lazy. It depends on the day whether I'd rather deal with the ones who at least want to help but haven't got a clue how, or the ones who just don't think I'm worth the effort.

Neither of them help much, though.

So for those who actually do want to help, here's a tutorial.

First of all, I get a whole lot of people who offer help. "Call me if you ever need anything." But as soon as they realize what "help" entails, they're gone. Of all the types, those are the people who do the most damage.

I can sort of brush off the ones who just ignore me as too self-centered or too lazy to care. And the ones who try to help and fail as just misguided.

But the ones who I think I can rely on, and then have to watch as they disappear--they confirm every belief that the illness feeds me. That I'm not worth caring about. Too much trouble. Too needy. Nothing more than a nuisance, not even worth the time of day.

So decide now. Being a friend to someone with mental illness isn't a cake walk. If you can't handle someone else's tears and pain, don't bother. If you don't have the guts to care no matter what, just leave.

If you do have the guts, though, make the commitment now. To stick with it. To actually care. To deal with the fear and the hurt and the odd habits and to make someone else a priority in your life. Anything less will only do more harm than good.

Anxiety makes it near impossible to trust. Especially social anxiety. And the prejudice around any mental illness makes it difficult to believe that anyone would actually help. I've heard the words "let me know if you need anything" so often that they're essentially meaningless to me anymore. I used to believe them. But I've been stung too often that way. And there are about two or three people in the world to whom I consistently answer the question "How are you?" honestly. To everyone else I lie through my teeth.

The people I learn to trust are the people who consistently show me proof that they care. Not the ones who drop by with flowers once and tell me to text them if I need them. The ones who go to the trouble of finding out that I love salmon pink roses and white chocolate, and make the effort to drop by consistently. Without a long drawn out conversation that will only do damage. The ones who don't just ask, "How are you doing?" and take my answer at face value, but actually treat me like a friend.

That means starting conversations about things other than my awful health.

If I feel like all you care about is finding out how horribly I'm doing and somehow fixing me, you can bet I'm just gonna ignore you to the best of my ability.

It takes time, to build that trust. It takes patience on both sides.

I've seen a few people who start down that path and then get offended the first time I turn down their party invitation or avoid questions about my health. They don't understand that I'm too terrified to do parties and too insecure to believe that they actually care about me after three conversations.

It's very few who stick at it long enough that when I need help I feel comfortable (translate as slightly less terrified) asking for it.

And it's very, very few who actually help once I ask for it.

Those very, very few are the ones who consistently respond to me. Not the ones who respond when they feel like it but ignore me or brush me off when they think they have something more important to do.

The ones who realize how much fear and self-hate and inner turmoil it took just to pick up my phone and send that text, and reassure me that they're glad I did.

The ones who are patient enough to not get angry when they can't seem to just talk me out of what seem to them like completely irrational fears.

The ones who seek out my company even when they know I'm not doing well, and who trust me enough to share their own feelings and doubts with me in kind.

The ones who still treat me like a friend even after they have seen my pain.

The ones who will simply sit beside me and watch Doctor Who with a box of tissues so that I don't have to be alone.

The ones who make the effort to know me well enough that they just laugh with me and offer a ride when I have to make a midnight run for the next random thing I'm craving to help with my migraine.

The ones who will just calmly remind me about the conversation we had the night before ECT that it's made me completely forget.

The ones who realize that they can't fix me any more than I can, but that just being there makes it so much easier for me.

In short, the ones who sincerely care about me enough just to do what they can to help without being annoyed or upset.

Those very, very few who make it that far are the ones who earn my undying loyalty and the ones who I treat in kind, whether that means staying up until five in the morning on a school night just to make sure they're safe and do my best to help. Or shipping stuffed animals across the country when they need something to cuddle and I can't be there. Or helping them pick the best shoes for a camping trip. Or listening to their music that I think is boring with them.

I've said before that most of those people, for me, have mental illnesses of their own. But they don't have to. Anyone can be that person.

Don't expect it to be easy.

But are my life and happiness worth your help? Are the life and happiness of someone you know worth your help?

If the answer is no, you need to seriously reconsider your priorities.

If the answer is yes, try to be that person, because you are very needed.

There are so many more people with mental illness out there than you think. We are everywhere. Every city. Every country. Every job. Every club. Every restaurant. Everywhere you look.

So be the help.

I know you're nervous. I know it's hard.

But just like everyone else, people struggling with mental illness just need love, pure and simple. A real friend. No big plans to magically fix things that can't be fixed. No judgment. Just a hand to hold and someone to laugh with. Someone who will bring a mint shake at two in the morning because they know I need one and I'm too ashamed to get it myself.

It IS hard, to see someone you care about hurt. It always will be. But loving someone with mental illness is no harder than loving someone with some other sickness. Sometimes it's extreme. Most of the time, it's not.

All it takes is a bit of humility, an open mind, and a willingness to try, and you could save a life.

Please try.

Nobody hears my screams for help over my fake smile.

CHAPTER TWENTY-SEVEN

OFTENTIMES, PEOPLE BELIEVE WHAT THEY WANT TO BELIEVE UNTIL THE TRUTH IS FORCED UPON THEM.

When I'm really bad, everything I do is a scream for help. Missing classes. Missing church. Flinching when someone calls my name. Clutching at my wrists. Hiding in my room all day.

People haven't really got a clue how to help, though.

To be fair, I don't entirely know how they can help either.

So instead of trying, they just look at my fake smile and my perfect grades and say, "oh, she's fine."

I'm not trying to blame anyone. It's really, really hard to help someone with severe mental illness. A few people try. Largely, they just make things worse.

But most people look at the fake smile that I can barely squeeze out and decide that I'm doing fine. I don't need help. Or I just need an extra pat on the back and another responsibility to pull myself together. Or some extra sermons on moral strength and repentance. Like making me feel unnecessarily guilty is going to help.

There are very, very few who actually offer realistic, useful help. Who see that I'm struggling and don't just brush it away based on the fact that I got out of bed and put on a dress and heels today. Who see that my problem is a medical one, not a moral one. And who treat me like they care, not like I'm another problem in their busy lives.

The world is making painfully slow progress toward treating mental health patients appropriately. At least nobody's ever drilled a hole in my skull, or tried to convince me that it's all because my uterus can't sit still . . . And I'm pretty sure I'm not a witch.

The word "stigma" itself comes from the term used in the late middle ages to describe the physical mark left on the body of a witch when she made a pact with the devil. Witches served as scapegoats for the plagues and dearths that decimated populations in late medieval times. Many of them were accused of witchcraft because they showed symptoms of mental illnesses, believed to be caused by demon possession or devil worship.

Nobody's ever tried to exorcise me. But the stigma is still strong.

I've never been chased out of town by a whip-carrying mob, but I've been effectively made to leave because I sought help for being suicidal.

There may not be chains in mental hospitals anymore, but the word "bedlam" still aptly describes life with mental illness. That word originates from the nickname of the first psychiatric hospital in England.

And even though churches have stopped preaching that "insanity" comes from sin, I'm still under a lot of pressure to shape up when the only wrong I've committed is being sick. Even from people very close to me.

I do my best to be open about my mental health. But it's incredibly difficult when it increases the pain and the judgment. As hard as I try not to, I'll probably keep forcing fake smiles out of self-preservation instinct forever. My need for help isn't going away, either. For the world of mental illness to change, it's time for the prejudice to disappear. Past time. Like, by at least a millennium.

And it's time for people to learn to see past the forced smile and the act and do something to help.

Communities pull together around other types of patients. They hold fundraisers and drop off freezer meals. Mental illness is just as real and can be just as severe. But even the people who can see through the stigma don't really know how to help.

So I'll write at least the things that work for me.

First of all, you can skip the suggestions. Believe it or not, a lifetime of mental illness has taught me a lot of the ins and outs. Unless I ask for specific suggestions, trying to tell me how to live a life that you know nothing about is really not going to help.

I've been told that I need to start running, that I should get into yardwork, that I should read a certain book or use a certain self-help program, that I should try anything from massages to meditation to extreme diets. And I've tried a lot of things. A LOT. And almost none of them have made a difference. I spend a lot of time researching and going over things with my doctors in order to decide what might actually help. And my parents spend a lot of money on new medications and sun lamps and water filtration systems and foods. When I'm really hurting, being told to try another useless thing just shoves me deeper into the blackness. I'm not sitting around waiting for a miracle, here. I'm fighting!

I should mention, too, though, that some of the few things that have actually helped me have come from talking to family members with similar problems. I greatly appreciate that. If we never shared ideas among the mental health community, we would never get anywhere.

What I object to is being bombarded with random suggestions, accompanied by the expectation that I will follow up, by people who have limited experience with what they're talking about. I often come out of a social encounter with a list of several "new" things that people want me to try, most of which I've either already tried or heard of and decided against. Some people will even follow up and ask if I've tried it yet, and then I have to explain that yes, I tried it two years ago and it did nothing.

If you truly know of something that breaks the mold, I have no objections to it being shared. But face-to-face social encounters are already super stressful for me. Maybe try an email. Or a text. Back it up. Send me a link to the research. And don't expect me to actually try it, or to follow up. If I tried every idea everyone gave me, I'd be trying so many new things at a time that I wouldn't be able to recognize which was working if one of them did.

One of my major problems with people trying to help is that they stomp all over my social anxiety.

She has severe social anxiety? Let's see, why don't we show up at her front door unannounced with a large group of people and see if she wants to spill her guts to us about something so personal she can't even face thinking about it in private? Perfect!

Once or twice I've had well-meaning church groups throw surprise parties or show up to sing happy birthday, and I end up just completely breaking down and having indignant people on my hands. Or people who want to help who think they can be my therapist and start asking me all about my mental illnesses.

I don't even do well with trained therapists, thank you very much.

I really, really, appreciate the people who want to show their support. But parties and unannounced doorbell rings feature in some of my worst nightmares. Right along with people who ask super personal questions when I barely even know them.

If you actually want to show your support, try leaving a plate of cookies or a stuffed animal with your number and a note offering help if you can ever do anything. I'm a whole lot more likely to text that person for help when I need it than ask any of the group who showed up at my door wanting to shower me in hugs and emotions.

A lot of people have this thing about hugs helping. Like the more physical contact I have with other people the inherently happier I'll be. I would be more comfortable with a slap in the face. Random people trying to give me hugs makes me fake needing the bathroom and hide in a stall until I can calm down enough to look someone in the eye without puking. It's the ultimate trap in an emotional situation, the thing that makes me panic every time.

I make a point of sitting on the end of the row nearest the door where I will be least likely to be noticed if I need to make a hasty exit. Also with my back to the fewest number of people. Sometimes people come swarm around me and try to talk to me and I'm running for the door before the class even begins.

If you actually want to help, you might try saying hi and sitting quietly next to me. Or better yet, running interference between me and everyone else. The relief when I can avoid talking to people I don't want to is enormous. And the person sitting next to me who talks to the crowd so all I have do is show off that fake smile is an angel.

I used to live in the most popular apartment in the area. Don't ask me how I got there. I ended up with the front door wide open, and an open invitation for everyone and anyone walking by to come in and play with my cat and share all the gossip. And a whole lot of parties.

I sincerely love to cook. But it also gave me a great excuse to hide during those parties. I could join in for thirty seconds and then run back to the kitchen to flip the donuts. And messes make me anxious. I can't stand the piles of dishes and flour and grease spilled all over the counters. So while the party is eating my donuts, I'm back in the kitchen cleaning until there's not a spot to be found.

Not much of a party, really. Tons of social anxiety. Pressure to be in the middle of it. Paying for the refreshments. And everyone either wanting to compliment my cooking or ask if they can try something with my cat, who is the star of every party. Her big, beautiful eyes could win over the staunchest dog person in the world.

You wanna do a party my way? Bring over a pizza, a bucket of ice cream, and a season of a history channel show. And ward off everyone else who wants to butt in. That with a single, good friend sounds second to as relaxed as I can get, which is really saying something.

If you're going to try to help, though, you'd better be prepared.

Relationships are generally a disaster for me. Neighbors, coworkers, roommates, classmates, they're all just a bad idea.

But the worst ones are the ones who offer to help, who think they can handle it, and then disappear. The ones who act like my friends as long as it doesn't get hard.

So don't offer to help if you can't deal with what that means.

And in the long run, the very best thing you can do is your homework.

Find out about mental illness. Realize that it's actually a real, medical problem, not just a figment of the imagination, or a sin or its punishment. It's a sickness like any other.

And then hear the screams. Understand that I need help, but don't assume you know how to offer it, because chances are you don't.

I was always too anxious to be a half-decent stage actor. Too scared of everyone watching me. In real life, I'm forced to put on a constant act. I'm not sure how many people I actually fool. But even through the act, those screams are there, in everything I do. Hear them. Respect them. And only then try to help.

Silence is the only option.

CHAPTER TWENTY-EIGHT

SOMEWHERE UNDER ALL THE PAIN I LIVE IN, I THINK I HAVE NORMAL DESIRES LIKE EVERYONE ELSE. I WANT TO GET BETTER. I WANT TO HAVE A JOB THAT DOESN'T INVOLVE TOO MANY SOCIAL SKILLS AND FIND A WAY TO HELP PEOPLE LIKE ME WHO ARE OVERWHELMED WITH ALL THE CONFUSION AND JUDGMENT OF MENTAL ILLNESS. I WANT TO GET MARRIED AND HAVE KIDS. I WANT TO BE ABLE TO TALK TO PEOPLE.

Right now, all I want is to curl up in a little ball. I don't want to write this sentence. I don't want to cuddle my cat. I don't want to eat, or breathe, or sleep, even. I want to die. So what do I do? I wander aimlessly around the house, bumping into walls, crying, digging my nails into my arms, and trying not to see everything around me as a weapon capable of taking my life.

On a normal day, my main desire is to avoid people. Panic sets in when a family member walks into the room. If I'm lucky, I might want to do something. Like draw, or go to the store. But mostly, no, all I want to do is avoid any sort of contact with almost every person I know until I can sleep, and then it starts all over again.

Mental illness does that. It swallows who I am. My hopes and dreams.

My personality. My talents. My relationships. I'm not entirely sure how I even know what I want in the long run, because those feelings surface only for a few seconds in very rare moments.

But I've been in psych hospitals. I've been dragged there in handcuffs. I've been forced to sit on an uncomfortable chair in uncomfortable clothes that don't fit for days. Praying with every grain of my existence just to not be alone in that horrible place anymore.

And psych hospitals are filled with people like me who don't know what they want. They know they don't want food. They don't want to read that boring novel, or see the long list of doctors every day. They don't want to spend another night in their uncomfortable, cold bed with lights from the hall shining through the doorless entrance.

Some, like me, are there because they desperately want to die. Some because they desperately want to be skinnier than their already skeletal bodies. Some because they simply can't take care of themselves, and nobody else is willing or able to help them. They desperately want for someone they love to come see them.

But mostly, everyone there spends their days staring at the walls in between answering the same painful list of questions to a list of doctors almost as long. They grudgingly participate in group therapy, and resignedly draw (with padded tools) or distractedly read an ancient book from the hospital's single shelf.

So many of us with severe mental illness have given up on life. The illness has taken our humanity, and the few, unobtainable desires left over come from the sickness, not from our hearts.

There are group therapy sessions there. Sessions with people who are just like me, who struggle just to stay alive under all the pain. Who don't really know what they want.

The therapists who lead those sessions normally have to pull words from patients like a dentist pulling teeth.

Yesterday my friend joked that being around people is so awful that we should start "Anxiety Anonymous." A place where anxious people can come to hide from the world, where all the chairs face outward at the blank wall and nobody talks, just sits in silence until they think they can face the real world again. I would go there!

One of the things mental illness seems sickeningly adept at demanding is silence.

The desire for silent anonymity outweighs even the other demands for death or sleep or skinniness.

Depression sucks away energy. There are instants when I can feel just enough normal emotion to desperately want someone, but I'm too exhausted to talk and too scared to tell anyone anyway.

Anxiety screams and whispers and pokes and prods until I am certain beyond all doubt that everyone I love hates me. The more I love someone, the more repulsive they find me. They don't want to hear me complain. They don't care if I'm hurting. If I died, they'd throw a party at my funeral. I'm nothing more than an annoyance to them. So instead I hide my fear. I keep my shaking hands shoved deep in my pockets and bite the inside of my cheeks to stop the tears from falling. And most of all, I keep my mouth shut.

Part of me knows that those thoughts are wrong, that they can't be true. At least, not completely. But the world disagrees. People seem to think that mental illness is something to be ashamed of. I should be ashamed of not being able to control my own thoughts. Ashamed of being needy and insane. It's my own fault that I can't get better. I'm not trying hard enough. What's next? Being so obsessed with my body image that I refuse to eat? Seeing things that aren't really there?

So what do I do? What do we do, stuck in group therapy, sitting in that far too brightly lit circle in uncomfortable chairs, trapped in living hell, not allowed to leave unless we can prove that we're stable enough not to be treated like a danger to society?

Some of us try to force ourselves to talk about the truth, going against every instinct screaming in our ears. Some make things up, just to affect the image of stability and calm long enough to be let out of this prison. But most just sit with lips glued together. Because silence is the only option. The only option that won't make everyone hate you more than they already do. The least terrifying of the very limited choices. The option that acts as a wall protecting you from even more scorn and ridicule.

I've trained myself now to be as open as I can about my illness. Because I know that the silence of people like me only makes the prejudice worse.

But every time I open my mouth to say anything that might make me more vulnerable I have to fight the pain in my stomach and the panic in the back of my brain.

Every word I write hurts, knowing that I'm giving people more reason to hate me.

I've trained myself to ask for help, too. Sometimes, it even helps. And sometimes all the twigs I've used to prop up my reasoning and hold back the terror and pain snap and everything avalanches on top of me and I can't work up the recklessness to ask again for weeks.

I'm going to ask of you, everyone reading this, something that I know will be incredibly difficult.

Silence is no longer the only option. There are people all over the country, all over the world, who struggle to live lives with mental illness, just like I do. But we can no longer afford to be silent. It's time for us to step up and speak out and show the world that we are here, that our illness is real and treatable, and that we deserve every consideration given to patients of any other disease.

We need, and deserve, the opportunity to move forward, to receive and reevaluate professional care. To not be trapped in psych hospitals against our wills, but to have the final say in our own treatments. To live life to the best of our abilities, whatever that means for each of us as individuals. And to never be judged based on our diagnoses rather than our actions.

So, everyone who has ever fought with your own mental illness. Everyone who has watched family or friends struggle. Everyone who has lost someone you love to mental health symptoms. All of us. Let's now pull together to fight the prejudice which is holding us back.

Please share, if you can, your own experience with mental illness, using #Don'tCallMeCrazy. Or simply any way that you can.

Let's prove to the world, and ourselves, that we have nothing to be ashamed of. Because we don't! We are not crazy. Just sick.

EPILOGUE

We had four weeks to notice something was wrong. It was the week before Christmas in 2020, the pandemic year. Social distancing kept everyone home. My husband and I were expecting our first child. In the coming week, I would celebrate my 23rd birthday, my 3rd anniversary, and of course, Christmas itself. It should have been a time of rejoicing, even in the midst of a social distancing.

We got the report from Mom that Jessica was behaving strangely. She was sleeping nearly constantly, always "busy," but never seeming to actually do anything, and had ceased nearly all social contact with her housemates (my parents and younger sister). On Friday, December 18th, Jessica talked to Dad and said that she and David Tennant had made a psychic connection and were getting married on Monday (you can't say she didn't have good taste!). It was schizophrenia, newly manifested in our attention. I found out on my birthday. I quickly felt a certainty that this would eventually take her life.

The next several weeks were difficult. It became clear that the Jessica we knew was very much not the one that we were seeing. Her articulate sentences turned to word salad. Her attentiveness and care for her mental health plummeted. She canceled an ECT session. She stopped taking meds. She sent texts about conversations that hadn't occurred, introduced Dad to people who weren't there. She wandered the house aimlessly. Her personality, so keen to help others and ease suffering, changed. She was too busy to see our younger sister's excitement in Jessica's Christmas gift to her. She argued with Mom and Dad. Words of encouragement turned to accusations and frenzied fears. On New Year's Eve, my husband and I heard a knock at our door. Jessica had called our local police station and told them that he was suicidal. He wasn't, and Jessica hadn't spoken to him in months. My husband shook for an hour after the officers left. Only a few days later, she alleged that he had abused her. Day after day, I saw people around me look at me like I was crazy when I told them of Jessica's stories. Her words didn't make sense.

About a week into the new year, she seemed to be improving. She sent out texts explaining that she was recognizing that she had experienced hallucinations and apologizing for harm she had caused. Her texts to me became much more normal, more logical. But then, in the early morning of January 13th, Dad walked down to his home office and saw her light on. He quickly called 911, but Jessica's life was already effectively over. Sometime in the night, she had sat on her bed, opened various medication bottles, and taken an unknown amount of their contents. She was taken by ambulance to a hospital and remained critical for nearly 24 hours. A ventilator and life support kept her alive, but she was getting worse. Finally her organs started to fail, and it was time to let her go. She passed from this world to the next on January 14th, 2021, at 3:25 AM.

Jess tried so hard to live her life as best she could. She tried to make memories with us. In her social anxiety and physical illnesses, she would take time to cook with us, explore new stores, debate controversies, laugh at cat antics, and stay close when others suffered. In the midst of her first suicide attempt, she was scared. She called for help. This time, she didn't. Weeks after her passing, we found a suicide note. It was calm, logical, and clear. If she regretted her final decision in life, she did not live to rue it. After a life filled with pain, she was finally free.

What do we learn? What can we do? There are some pains too deep to understand, some wounds too big to sew back together. We can ask others to stay, for us, and most people can be asked to stay for themselves. Most lives will get brighter. Most days will improve. Suicide does not give time to heal. No matter how much brighter the earthly days ahead, they all go dark with death. But I can't blame Jessica, or anyone. She fought for light. She starved for it. We don't know her final thoughts and feelings, but I have to believe that she could no longer see a brighter future. She had explored every avenue. The most brutal last-resort treatment for her depression, dozens of medications, holistic treatments. She tried therapy. She tried faith. And in the end, she couldn't make it stop. Even in her death, she seemed attentive to others. It seems she chose the method she thought would be least traumatic to us.

We preach against suicide. We tell people that tomorrow needs them. It is almost always true that suicide is not the answer, but how much can a human heart take? My whole family is weeping today, but tomorrow we'll smile. Her pain hurt us all deeply. It was hard to see her suffer. In a way, this frees us all.

It is interesting this world we live in. Our concepts of pain and life are not always reasonable. I think de Cartes may have been confused by Jessica's struggle. "I think, therefore I am"--but what if it is no longer you doing the thinking? Jessica had become her own worst nightmare. She could no longer recognize truth from fiction. After defending others from pain her entire life, she was inflicting deep damage on others. She had fights with our parents. She accused others. She ignored calls for attention and love. Was there any answer left? Mental illness had overpowered all influence she may have once yielded over her existence, the tenuous control she had tenaciously gripped for two long decades. She--our Jessica--was no longer thinking. We had lost her to the sea.

You've doubtless heard it before. When a horse breaks a leg, we shoot it. "But," we reason, "human lives are more valuable and sentient than animal lives." Nevertheless, when a cancer patient has fought a good fight, we say, "If your remaining quality of life will be improved and you so wish, it's alright for you to stop fighting. You have our respect in your decision to die." We let them choose, effectively, a prolonged suicide. We smile when they pass and say, "They're no longer in pain. It's what they wanted. Their body was a cage they are now free from." But when your mind is the cage, we say, "You must stay. You cannot leave. Your attempts to die will be fought at every turn. And you cannot stop treatments. No matter what effect they have on you, even if they destroy you, you have to keep trying. You cannot stop." How can that be right?

If there is anything that Jessica's words in this book teach us, it's that each case is different. She shows us her mind in stunning detail. In my own battles with mental illness, I have seen in myself many of the experiences and emotions she expressed. But my illness lessened. Hers got worse. You could say that she had an emotional cancer, aggressive and metastasizing. Reader, your life is yours. I would ask you to stay. Stay here. Stay for tomorrow's sunshine. Stay to see past yesterday's rain. Most cancers can be healed, at least for a while. Most mental clouds lift. You may well find a time when your fight is easy, or gone completely. Please consider it. Search for the hope in the future. Especially if your fight is still young, give your all in the effort before accepting defeat. You may yet find a victory, unforeseeable from your current valley. But in the end, you choose how to stay. Your illness is not the same as that of Jessica, or your friend or roommate or favorite celebrity. Perhaps, as Jessica says, the fight against self-harm and suicide is a desperate battle for self-preservation. She was no longer the person she knew, and today I think that she won the war. She reclaimed, in death, the control over her destiny that she had lost in life. But she also lost the chance to share in the future. My unborn child will never know his aunt. She'll never in life see his smile, hear his laughter. She will never again on this earth be able to share herself with others. In other words, her final self-preservation left her utterly and completely alone. She saved herself, but only herself. She will never again be present in life to aid in the preservation of others.

Your story does not need to end the same as hers. You get to choose for yourself. You are not alone. Many thousands of others have felt pain like yours. You are not crazy. Your feelings are not imagined. But today, and tomorrow, take a moment to think of where you belong. Where are you needed? Do you need to be here tomorrow, for your current or future children? For your friends? For dreams that you still haven't fulfilled and for smiles not yet seen? Choose carefully. There is a hefty price to pay when you decide to make a choice your last.

www.ingramcontent.com/pod-product-compliance
Lightning Source LLC
Chambersburg PA
CBHW071227170426
43191CB00032B/1073